1. violent or aggressive behavior w
    involving the violent abuse of a

* * *

"One's dignity may be assaulted, vandalized and cruelly mocked, but it can never be taken away unless it is surrendered."
— Michael J. Fox

CONTENTS

Acknowledgments

Mickey Conley

Jessie E. Koehler

Maleeka Hollaway-Willie

Marybel Carmona

Malcolm Robins

Chris C.

Anoushka Santinelli

Carol T.

Anonymous

E. Marie

L. P.

Leah Hughes

Ashely Morgan

Gail P.

Lily Rose

Natalia Hardly

Stephie T

Catherine Percival

Monique Alvisse

L. C.

Jane Frank

Prometheus Unbound

J. B.

Laura Markle

Teri Lyn

Freeda Knight

Elise Montgomery

In the Mind of an Abuser

Amberlee Hoagland

Statistics

Safety Plan

When I Leave I Should Have

Resources

I Got Flowers Today

ACKNOWLEDGMENTS

Many thanks to the brave hearted who submitted their inspiring stories, of love, loss and powerless vulnerability.

May you always have peace knowing you are free, strong, and beautiful just the way you are.

* * *

Domestic Violence is a silent epidemic. Women are all too comfortable, taking the abuse, rather than standing up for themselves, out of fear and humiliation. Women, just like myself, feel like the abuse it their fault, That they are the ones who need to change. They feel like they can fix their abusers, to love them out of whatever haunts them. One-third of female homicide victims, that are actually reported, are killed by an intimate partner. In homicides where an intimate partner was killed, no matter man or woman, 70% of the time the man physically abused the woman before the murder. Children who witness domestic abuse is the strongest risk factors for transmitting violent behavior from one generation to the next. In fact, Boys are twice as likely to abuse their own partners and children when they become adults… We create our children's hell.

* * *

I met my first husband when I was 22, in a bar (the worst place to meet someone). He was way older than me, like 21 years older, As a matter of fact, he was a year older than my dad. A lot of people said I was dating him to replace the father I was missing in my life. He was always the life of the party in every bar we went to. I would hear people talk nice to his face then talk about him behind his back. Over time people started telling me he was a bad seed. He was always in and out of jail into drugs and fights a lot. I also found out he had 9 kids. I never seen that until we got married. His kids were accepting of me, except his older two daughters because one was a year older than me the other was 6 months older than me.

About 5 months into our relationship, I got pregnant, and come to find out, a few weeks later he had also been with his ex-wife and she was pregnant too. She had her daughter in August, I had our son in October, so that made 11 kids. Well for the first two years of our sons life I went through "it's not mine" or "it isn't my dad's". When we met I already had a son who was a little over a year. He did not like my son and, no excuse, but being young, my son's father talked me into letting him raise our son (a mistake). It wasn't long until he went to jail. I could not afford to bail him out so when he got out, I was everything but a white woman, (old saying) and he pushed me into a wall, left, and went to the bar. I should have left right then. He was never getting married, he started screwing around with other women while I was at work, and he never held but one job the whole 12 years we were together. I caught him in the act in my own house but he pulled this "it wasn't what you think" with her head bent over the back of the arm chair, face up and his penis down her throat. I decided to leave him, and got me an apartment where the manager kept sneaking in my apartment trying to put moves on me, so I moved in with my sister down the street from him. He had thrown my son and I's stuff out on the porch, and said he was in love with this college girl because, "they had so much in common" (drugs, music, and sex).

    A month or so went by, he started trying to wind me back, and eventually I went back because I was thinking this was real. Well about two weeks later, he went to jail for a probation violation. While he was in jail, he got in some trouble, next thing I knew he was calling wanting to get married and give our son his last name. So stupid me, said yes. We got married in the local jail and a couple weeks later had our sons last name changed. About a year into the marriage, he told his friends he only had our sons name changed because that's the only way he could get me to marry him, and he needed me to marry him so I wouldn't be able to testify against him when he went to court.

    Once he got out, for about the first year and a half, it was great. Everything I was wanting was happening. That was short lived. He was staying up all night for days. I did not know about meth at the time. I was coming home from work every day, and I would have a house full of people they be smoking stuff and sucking stuff up through a straw in their nose. I knew better than to ask so I would take my son out of the swing or playpen most of the time and go to my room because they would all be in the kitchen. After about a week I didn't want all these people in my house so I told him. He had been up like 5 or 6 days. I was fixing supper. He came in and said "you need to try this" I said no. After saying no ten, times he grabbed my face and put it in a pile of it, of course, I was hot, and I ended but being up until I went to work the next day. No matter how hard I tried to sleep. I was tired when I got home, and he was watching TV . I went into the bathroom took shower. He came in and forced me to have sex. He was like a whole different person. He raped me. He sodomized me. He cut me with a pocket knife (superficial), and tried to put his whole hand up inside me. I screamed. He got mad because my scream woke up our son.

A couple months down the line I was so sick I could hardly get out of bed. I ended up losing my job. I decided to go to the doctor after a few days, that is when I found out I was three months pregnant. I started having strange people coming to my home around 11 p.m.-1 a.m. to party with my husband. His daughter let it slip a couple days later, that the couple coming to my home, was major meth dealers, and the guys were coke dealers. He was telling everyone I was pregnant. About 2 months later, I was cooking supper, he had been up 7 or so days, and he wanted something to eat. So I fixed our sons plate then his. His daughter had come to eat with us. I forgot his milk and he yelled "bring my milk" I said 'I am busy give me a minute'. I heard his daughter say does she know you are putting coke in her drinks. He said 'no, she is too stupid'. It made me so mad I took that glass of milk into him slammed it on the table it splattered everywhere and this is when the hitting started. He threw the glass plate at me, jumped over coffee table slammed me into the wall tried kneeing me in the stomach, and holding his hand over my mouth and nose till I almost passed out. He told me to be a woman and stand up. My son was crying. He was saying stuff like 'Look at your whore mom, our mom is worthless, your mom is a coke whore, daddy will show you what mommy needs', and threw me into our huge chair when I fell out he picked it up and threw it down on me. I must have passed out for a moment or two because I heard yelling and it was his daughter yelling "Dad stop. She is pregnant. Are you fucking stupid?" He grabbed her by her hair and threw her outside and told her to stay out of his business. Then he raped me again in front of my year and a half old son. He pushed me towards my son and was telling me to feed the semen that was all over me to our son.

I had no clothes on because he tore them off, so I grabbed a dish towel, went to the bedroom, got me some clothes, and washed myself off. A couple hours later my son went to sleep. He had left while I was getting my son to sleep. He came in and went to sleep on the couch and slept for almost 2 days. Then after that this was an every week thing he would stay up 6 days, and sleep on the 7[th,] then repeat. Well he ended up in pain one day that brought him to his knees (loved every minute of it). I took him to the ER, found out he had gallstones, and had to have surgery. On the way home from the hospital he was in a lot of pain every bump he would smack me in the head all the way home (40 min drive). When we pulled up he slammed my face in the steering wheel and said "Hurts don't it bitch"? My nose and lip bled for a minute. Only if he knew I hit every bump on purpose.

He had missed a probation meeting because of the surgery and they showed up to arrest him. They gave him a second chance until the next day. He flunked the test and they took him to jail from there. He ended up doing 2 years to 1. While he was gone I ended up having the baby which made 12 kids for him. He got mad cause I couldn't afford to come see him every weekend.

I was staying with my sister to save money. I finally got my own place was doing really good. On Jan 2nd I went to get kids, and my baby had died of S.I.D.S. He ended up getting released for the circumstances. I was a basket case. He never held the baby because he was locked up, so it did not affect him the way it did me. Once home he wanted to know where the baby passed. I pointed to the couch and he asked if we could have sex. That puzzled me. Our son passed away today and you want to have sex where he took his last breath, are you freaking serious. I said to him "does it look like I want sex?" and of course the verbal abuse started. I was cheating etc. My sister had called the family doctor and got me some nerve medication and brought the prescription over he was crushing these pills and putting them in my tea and Pepsi. I was so out of it, I fell asleep at the funeral home making arrangements. I got smacked when we got home because I went to sleep. So two days later was the viewing. We walked in, and I lost it. He gave me a pill, and I took it to calm me down. He told me "if you don't quit being so dramatic and quit that damn crying, I will slap the dog shit out of you when we get home." We went home and my mom, dad, stepmother and brother came back to the trailer. He told them they needed to leave they were upsetting me. So at the funeral the next day he was inviting everyone to go to the local bar that evening. it wasn't until years later I was told by my mom and friend that they seen him put a bunch of powder stuff in my orange juice at the funeral.

I couldn't take off work to long. Someone had to support my son, so I went back to work two days after the funeral. I worked a couple days then on the 3rd day I received in the mail, a bible in a wooden stained box with my sons name and picture on it from my step mother, along with pictures from Christmas. I got teary eyed and went to the bathroom to cry, when I came out to go to work there was two men sitting at my table. He said they were going to play cards, and to give him money so he could go to the store while I was at work. I did. I went to work and made it to the parking lot and could not bring myself to go in. I finally went to the office and they told me to go home and take whatever time I needed.

I went home, and there he was with drugs. He spent all my money. When he asked why I was home, I tried to explain, of course no sympathy from him. I sat in the rocker and he wanted me to borrow money off my family. I told him hell no and he said "well if all you are going to do is sit there and ball like a damn baby, leave or go to your room". I told him I don't have to go nowhere this is my house. If I want to cry I will, and he kicked the chair over, pulled me up by my hair, smashed my face on the wall going down the hallway, and pushed me in my room. Next thing I know I hear him spanking (hard) on our son. I came down that hallway like a mad bull. I said "What the hell do you think you are doing" he said "He shit his pants" I said "Because of you, you scare him" he said "Take pussy boy and yourself back to that room and stay there" (now I have a house full and no one is saying a word) I said 'I am leaving', he said 'The hell you are'. He wouldn't let me out so I finally just took my son and went back to my room. I went back to work the next day because, I had to feed and take care of my son. He promised (should have known better) he was done with the drugs and I was glad.

In March I worked second shift, so I got home about 11:30 p.m. I asked where my son was he said at his sisters and he was waiting for me. He told me to follow him to his sisters (right down the street) so I did. When we got there my son was asleep on the couch. Sitting around the table I noticed they were smoking something. I asked what is was I was told it was crack. I got mad and took my son to my sister's house and left him there. When came home, he gave it to me, and I smoked it. I did this (not in the presence of my son he was never there) for about 2 months on the weekend. It got to the point, I realized the pain is still there. I need to deal with it and told him no more, he said ok.

Things seemed fine until July, I was getting ready for work. I hear a commotion outside, looked out the window, and I saw these men in like ninja outfits running by my trailer didn't think anything until they busted in my door (my son is 3 so picture this). They came down the hall into the bathroom threw me and my son both on the ground yelling for my husband. I said he was gone went to town they had shot guns to me and my sons head. After making my son wet himself and them capturing my husband down the road they finally let us go. He finally went to prison for 6 years (6 do 3). I filed for divorce after a few weeks he would call and beg not to do this he will change blah, blah, blah. Even though he was in prison he was still verbally abusive. If I wasn't there when he called he would call all my family, and start cussing at them. So I decided to put the divorce on hold (mistake). He got a modification and was released. After about four months being out he was diagnosed with stage two tonsil cancer. He had to have a massive surgery. It was a 10 hour surgery, and he ended up with a trachea. You would think in his position he would be nice, hell no!!!! He was in the hospital for 9-10 days. The whole time he was up there, I would be there. When no one was there with us, he would give me the finger, write on the erase board profanity, tell me to die, to leave, etc. He started to throw stuff at me like ice water pitchers, coffee cups, and whatever else he could grab because I couldn't understand him sometimes. It would get bad enough where the nurses would send me home. He did not want me to sleep and he was so mean. I would get home (45 min away) and the nurse would call and say he wants me to come back. So I would get back in the car and go back. If I took too long, he was nasty.

Once he got home things were better after a few months. I thought he had changed then people started telling me he was back on drugs. One night I was upstairs in my room on the computer. I heard screaming down stairs and someone yelling for me I went down and it was a good friend of mine. She told him "you either tell her or I will " he said "Go ahead" and as he was telling me he was back on drugs and dealing, he opened the door and threw her out into our bushes. She called me the next day and told me where he was keeping it, and I found it. I questioned him when he got back, he tried denying it but when I showed him he went outside. I heard my son scream, the door opened and my son came flying across the room (literally). I jumped up and I fought like a momma bear fighting for her cub. I wasn't taking it anymore and I wasn't doing this either. I grabbed my son and went to a friend's house and filed a protective order the next day. Before I got back home the cops were already there making him leave. The last hit I got was during the last stages of the divorce which took almost 2 years. He busted my windshield out, lied in court about that and scared the witnesses that were there to testify. I went to get my sons movie where he was staying (a mutual friend and her husband) and he was writing the judge. I made the comment "Grow up and quit writing over stupid shit." He jumped up from the couch and busted my face with the back of his hand. I left, and went home with this big mark across my face, and small cut under my right eye. I told my friend I needed to go to store, and I'll be back in 10 minutes. When I got back there was a state cop at my house. He saw my face, and went across parking lot to where he was staying. My husband tried to say I was beating him up, but he had no mark whatsoever. I swore no man will ever treat me or my kids like that as long as I live, and I meant it.

I've since remarried. He is a good man. Good to my kids and he works. Till this day, intimate relations is still hard, because certain words, positions, and actions triggers my past. I take things day by day. But I am a survivor!

♛ **Survivor: Mickey Conley**

* * *

I met my first husband back in 1982. We had worked at the same place. He always seemed like a true gentleman at work. We became close friends and soon began to date. It all seemed so nice I thought I had finally met the man I would spend the rest of my life with. We became engaged within a year. My family loved him, and also thought we were a perfect match. I was so happy. After we married we soon had our first child and suddenly things changed. He was not the man I married.

First came the verbal abuse, then I was not allowed to leave the house without him or even use the phone to call my family. Then the hitting began. It occurred on a daily bases. Of course he would always apologize, and promise to never to do it again, yet there was always a next time. I began to think there was something wrong with me, and what could I do to change this. But of course, there was nothing I could do. It got worse. Several times he almost killed me and on one occasion he almost killed my mother for trying to save me.

I will share a couple of my terrifying experiences with you. First experience: I was always to bring him a glass of ice water when he was thirsty. On this one occasion he got angry because I had not put enough ice in the glass, so he knocked the glass out of my hand and began yelling that I was just a 'stupid idiot', and could do nothing right. He then kicked me in my face and spit on me several times. I began to bleed all over the floor and was thrown onto the broken glass he threw. As he kept yelling 'you can't even clean this up right' and continued to beat me.

I also made the mistake of telling him it was gross for him to use our drinking glasses as a spittoon and he said 'do you really want to see what is gross?' And he then forced me to drink his entire glass that he had been spitting in.

I so clearly remember most of the events that occurred however some I did push back in my subconscious. The abuse occurred for years, we were only married a few years, but the abuse lasted through the separation, and even after the divorce, as he continued to follow me and stalk me. It finally stopped after twelve years when his health was failing due to several strokes, alcohol, and drug use.

The day I did leave me and my 3 sons left with nothing, as we had to make a quick escape. My mother came and got us. But the next day when we thought he would be at work, we decided to take a ride over to the house and get some things for the boys. As we were rushing around trying to grab diapers, clothes, toys or whatever we could, he came home. He was so angry he threw me down on the couch and began beating me. My mother then grabbed a frying pan and began hitting him with it, yelling at him to stop. He then turned around and grabbed her and began choking her. I was trying to pull him off my mother, when he heard a noise and he stopped. We ran out of the house with the kids and escaped with just a few things. But we were alive!

Sadly I did not get much help from the police. The laws then were not there to help victims of Domestic Violence, and even though they say they have improved I do not agree. Too many women are feeling alone and abandoned.

It has been a long time since these events occurred, and I will say it took years to heal from it. But it can be done. Now I can easily talk about it. I have the vivid memories but the pain and anger are both gone. I myself am a true believer in the healing power of God, He is my strength. I do believe that our past experiences make us who we are today. I once thought I was a loser and could never do anything, as I was told this on a daily bases. But I have achieved most of my goals in life. Got an education in a few things. I hold a PhD in Religious Education, and I am currently an EMS Instructor. And recently written a book I had published, so I say this to let other ladies to know, when your abuser tells you that you are stupid and cannot do anything, that is a lie! You can do anything, for you are a strong and smart woman.

♛ **Survivor: Jessie E. Koehler**

* * *

This is my story. I never thought I would have a "story" but that goes to show you how life has a way of flowing against your plans. I met my husband in April of 2009. At the time I was 19 and a manager at a fast food restaurant. I thought I was on top of the world. Being the youngest manager in the state, at the time, I had reason to be cocky or at least that's what I made myself believe. Upon first seeing him, I thought nothing of it. He worked beneath me, and that was that. Until one day, in general conversation with my crew, he asked me my age, and called me a " little girl" and that boiled my blood. But it also made me notice him. Needless to say, I kindly cursed him out and vowed I would never speak to him again, to "prove" my adulthood.

One day, he decide he was going to call out of work, on my shift, and I refused to wash one dish, so I went and picked him up, from home…and the rest was history.

I had never been attracted to a street man one day of my life. But this guy was tall, dark, handsome, with dimples, had charisma, and more than that he had a dream, and THAT'S what caught me more than anything. We grew up two completely different ways- me, the suburbs of Atlanta, GA -him, the hood of Huntsville, AL and that caused issues down the line. I can say it was a whirlwind thing! We started out as a coworkers with benefits, and next, we were "in love". So much happened between then and the first incident. I ignored all the signs... not necessarily that he was abusive, but that this was not the man for me.

We eloped...May 17... one week later, it happened. I can't even remember what the argument was about but he pushed me into the wall, the ironing board was propped up on the wall, he pushed me so hard it broke. Through all the screaming, I managed to catch the look in his eyes, and I did not recognize the man I married. I was packing to go on a weekend family visit with my sister and he took the suitcase and literally threw it on top of me. I could not for the life of me understand what would make a man so mad. For him to treat a woman this way. I had a few scratches on my neck, when my sister noticed she asked what happened...and what did I do? I lied. Told her something bit me and I scratched it too much. That wasn't the first lie I would tell.

When I got back in town, he cried.. apologized.. I told him he had to leave...but I had just married him, and I wanted to save face for the decision I made, so I let him stay. A month later, I found out I was pregnant. I was terrified. Throughout that pregnancy, it got worse. I remember one time him slapping me so hard, I flipped over the couch, landed on my face, and all I could think about was my child. He then waited for me to get up, grabbed me by my neck, and told me, if I left him, he would kill me. I believed him.

A few months later, during another intense argument, he spit on me. And I never felt as low as I did then. That was my worst moment. I remember literally wishing death on him. Better yet, I would try to kill him. And even then, I didn't leave.

We separated multiple times after that. The abuse never stopped. At one point I got abusive back. A lot of times, my words were the abuse, as his were his hands. Choked unconsciousness, slapped, bitten, pushed, punched, you name it, I felt it. This went on for four years. Pure chaos. Many times I had to send our daughter to relatives for months to 'get myself together' only to know, I needed a way out. I could have easily left though. I was the one making the money. I had the car. But I did not want to experience the embarrassment of letting everyone know, I made a bad decision. That I had messed up.

There were a few friends around during those times who knew a little of what was going on. They urged me to leave or at least seek help for him and I. They were always there when I called, but none of them could make the decision for me. My absolute breaking point did not come until the final 4th year when I discovered that he had sex with another woman in our home, and it was a mutual friend. The physical abuse had not happened in a year, but the mental flashbacks and all the foolishness that had occurred since meeting him, had me fed up to capacity. That was the last straw. I took my daughter, left and never looked back.

During those years, we talked multiple times about the demons that haunted him from his childhood. Broken home, not knowing his father, never feeling good enough, the story of a black man who has never been told, he could do whatever he wanted to put his mind to. And somehow, I believed I could heal a lifetime of pain for him. I was wrong. He admitted he had an anger problem, and said multiple times that I reminded him of his mother, whom he has a strained relationship with. Deep down I knew he was a good person because he showed me he could be. He often cooked, cleaned, made money appear out of thin air, and he had other children he took care of, before our child was born. And when she came along, I went back to work, and he was Mr. Mom and was damn good at it. But no matter how good he was, he had issues that I could not fix.

I grew up in church, but during those 4 years I knew religion but had no relationship with God. But I can say, it's because of God I finally had the strength to leave. And leave without killing him or myself. I remember praying for three days straight after I left because the pain I felt was agonizing. I could not understand why God would allow me to go through so much and still not have good results. After the third day, waking up, I felt a strength I didn't know I had. It's amazing to me that I stayed in a dead situation so long just to keep from looking like a fool. Many times, he could have killed me, and I knew he tried, but out of stubbornness, I kept going back. I can't say I didn't love him, because love is unconditional and I loved him unconditionally, and I still do. I just know without any doubt that he was never meant to be with me forever. But just to teach me a lesson! I prayed that God would heal my heart…And I have forgiven him. The only way I could be happy was to forgive him, and its God who allows me to do that.

A few months later, I stood up in front of about 100 people on a Sunday morning, including my family, and I told my story. Some of my family members cried the whole time because they had no idea I went through this. Some were enraged and out for blood. A few people told me, that I had a gift for speaking in front of people, and that my story would save peoples' lives. I never saw it that way. When I go into details of my experiences, people cry and ask me "how am I so strong" and I have to tell them, it's not me by any means, it's ALL God! Prayer and faith change things and make a world of difference! But thanks be to God, I am alive and well since leaving, I have graduated from a HBCU with an undergraduate degree and I am enrolling in graduate school next semester. I am healthy, happy, and most of all I know my worth.

👑 **Survivor: Maleeka Hollaway-Willie**

* * *

Fifteen years ago I met a man I thought would be my prince charming, a person who. I thought, I could spend the rest of my life with. I remember it like it yesterday, hanging out with my cousin walking through downtown into the north end of my hometown in CT. I was having a conversation with my cousin, I passed a group of guys and I overheard one particular guy say to us 'Stop telling stories'. I stopped and looked at him and told him mind your business. He glanced at me, and apologized, so I continue my way. My cousin and I arrived at home, but forgot we still needed to go to the store. We decided to take the same path we took to go to the corner store, as I entered the store, I saw the same guy. I went to purchase my things and he stopped the cashier and paid for it. I was surprised. He then asked me if he could have my number. I stared at my cousin, and just stared back. Silly me, I gave him the number. I left the store one block down, my pager was blowing up. I got home and called the number back and it was him. We had long conversation which made me feel he really understood me and I could possibly see a future. He was quite a charm. He was very smart, funny, understanding anything a woman would desire. I started getting closer, hanging out with him meeting the family and pretty much building a relationship.

A year after I started seeing the change. There was times I just wanted to be by myself or maybe hang out with my friends. He wouldn't let me go to see my family and friends, arguing over little things, following me, keeping my pager. There's times I would visit and wouldn't let me go home. I started asking myself why am I letting him control me? I thought I was in love, silly me. I guess I did fall in love with this man who turned out to be demanding, controlling and vicious. I remember seeing him upset. He had his days if he didn't smoke weed he would be a great pain. I worked and at times had to help him with his habits, sad at times I would get upset. A man who used to take care of me, and once spoil me, now I'm the one taking care of him.

One day, I was tired from a long day working at the bank. I just wanted to go home and rest. My pager was going off non-stop. I finally answered before leaving work. It was late, as I worked second shift. I was tired. He was acting crazy. This is the day I should have walked away, but I didn't. Listening to him asking me to come over, he needed me and he was furious I didn't answer him quick enough, I tried to explain myself telling him I only get a short break. He shouted 'Are you cheating on me?' I told him he was wrong and I would call him tomorrow, and hung up. Once my shift was over, and as I was leaving the building, I heard a shout, it was him I walked over to the car and he got out and said come on, I asked him where we were going and he said to his house. I asked how will I get back home, and he told me he would get me a cab. I decided to get in the car, his friend dropped us off at his house, and as I walked thru the back of the bldg he started yelling, asking me why I hung up? I told him I was at work. That was the first time he punched me across my face ripped my shirt pulled my pants off to smell me. I was scared I began to yell he started to choke me. I remember kicking and crying, that's all I remember until I woke up on his bed with him looking over me, and him saying he thought I would never wake up. He kept me for three days, I lost my job. I just wanted to get away. He cried and told me he was sorry he just couldn't be away from me, and he would never do it again. I gave him the benefit of the doubt, he was nice for a couple of days, then he went right back to himself.

If I managed to get away he would follow me, make a scene, and stalk me. He knew what hole I would curl up and hide. I really was tired of it all. Isolated from the world, scared, and didn't have anyone to turn too. My family really didn't care. They were scared of him, and it came to the point I didn't have no one talk too, or anywhere to run. I decided to leave him, despite this, it was getting out of control. The hitting and the abuse physically, mentally, and emotionally was getting too much to bear, and was making me physically ill. I called my last resort my brother and his wife. I can trust his wife she never gave me a reason not too. She always understood me, and helped me in any way she could, so I called Sarah and she told me I could stay with her until I was ready to get on my feet, she knew how overwhelmed and tired I was of having to hide from my once prince charming, who now had become my stalker.

I was laying down on the couch. I wasn't feeling to great depression took over me, so I'd been throwing up for awhile. Sarah told me I should get checked, maybe a pregnancy test too. I was completely in my zone, tired and I heard a knock but who would have thought it was going to be for me. I started to doze off again, Sarah was in the shower, I was awakened by my brother Telling me I had to talk to HIM, and that he had told him I was there with them. My heart dropped. After hiding for several days, I thought I was safe. I was wrong. I heard him yelling I came to the hallway, he looked at me trembling, and told me to come back home with him, I told him no and that I was tired of the abuse and wasn't going through it again. He started begging me, tried to pull me close, as he talked I could smell liquor all over his body. I said no again and turned to enter the house, I felt a sharp pain. He had taken the bottle of Hennessey, and hit me on the head with all his might. I fell onto the ground, he then got on top of my chest and began to strangle me. I heard voices. Sarah began to yell. I was slipping. I heard people yelling, 'Her eyes are rolling back..' Then I passed out. I woke up gasping for air he has choked me so bad I had urinated on myself. As I came too, I felt one kick to my head, and another to my chest. He wasn't going to leave me alone. He began to strangle me again, it took 3 powerful women to fight him off of me. As I slowly started coming back, not even once I saw my brother helping me, the only face I saw was Sarah and two others. Everything happened so fast .Sarah manage to get him out of the building, I knew I wasn't safe for them for me to stay there anymore. I had to leave.

Having no one to run too, I went back. Days went by and I was back with my predator, he's no longer prince charming. I wasn't feeling to good, so I decided to check with my doctor why I was so sleepy. My pregnancy test was positive. Three months later, I found out I was having twins. I decided to keep them. I became real close to my provider, she wasn't only a doctor to me she became my way out. The predator wasn't too happy. He was upset, and felt i was trying to trap him. Truth is I trapped myself ,but just knowing I had the best of two souls in me, I just couldn't get a abortion. Feeling them inside me gave me hope and made me realize I can move on. Well so much for moving on, he continue hitting me, but every time I went with a injury to the doctors she wasn't hearing that. I finally asked my doctor. I asked her if she had a friend and she was pregnant, and has no one to help her, but is with a man that beats her, and she's scared how can I help her?. Dr Allen left the room. My heart was heavy. I was scared. I just knew she was going to call DCF. She came back in and said she canceled her appointments, lets talk. She asked if my 'friend' was me. I didn't answer her. I was so scared. Dr Allen said enough is enough. You have came in with several injuries, You're in danger, and I can no longer see you getting hurt. There's a way out! She gave me some pamphlets and a 1800 hotline number. She asked me to pack a backpack with my birth certificates and important documents, clothes, and a set of my keys, and to leave it at someone's house, or hide it in the house. She told me to start a diary, and not to keep it at the house. Dr Allen was the reason I survived. I began calling the hotline getting info, planning. I did exactly what she said. I hid my journal at my mom's house. Told a friend, in case something happened to me, where to find it. I was planning my way out.

I got wrapped up in thinking we could be a family so I stayed but still kept my diary and bag in a safe place. He continued to beat me I would pray to god which was my last resort. I cried my nights away, and ask god to help me, he became more involved in the drugs. He even became abusive with my twin boy, saying only the girl was his not the boy, I didn't care I would take blows when it came to my son I started fighting back. Although I'm a woman, but I wasn't going to let him touch my boy. I remember the last two beatings really awoke me. It was a Sunday. My baby boy was born dead, and they revived him and brought him back to life. He was a slow learner, he was diagnosed with ADHD and was always real sick with asthma, I almost lost him to meningitis.

My baby boy was only 7 years old it was my birthday, and I decided to take him to go pick up the kids, and go to dinner at friends. I was super excited. Mr. predator, hating going anywhere and always had to fight with me about going anywhere. It was a beautiful day, I was super excited and went to pick up the kids, to my surprise they were picked up by their father. I found it strange, I called him no answer. I went home to see if he had went back to the house. They were there, as soon as I walked in I saw a problem. My son was sitting at the table scared and crying. He was yelling at him. Calling him stupid. My daughter sat there quiet. I tried to take the kids by myself to eat and go to the movies. He began to insult me, calling me all names in the book. I ignored him, I wasn't going to let him ruin my birthday. I went to get a change of clothes for my kids, as I came out their room, I was surprised with a hot bucket of water, followed by a blow to my face. He ripped my dress off and put it in the bathtub with bleach, my day was ruined. I heard my babies cry, he hit me then strangled me in front of my babies.

I remembered what Dr Allen told me. I said that's it. Today is the day. I was so hurt I took my babies and my bible and began to pray just knew God would help me, he left for a few minutes. I checked my checklist, and I was ready to run. I cleaned myself up, I had blood all over my naked body from a busted lip. I grabbed my babies and a frozen pizza and waited for the time to escape. A half hour later, he came back and I was already in the couch with my babies he wouldn't stop threatening me. The truth is, I was tired from arguing. I must have fell asleep. I woke up choking and gasping for air. It was a weird smell, I have severe asthma funny that's what saved my life that day.

I was choking. I woke up. T.V wasn't on. My mouth was ducked taped hands, feet, and my kids were next to me, my head was on fire! I was burning. I looked up, and there he was in the corner of the living room laughing, and telling me you will never do your hair again. I squirmed around moving my legs hands and trying to scream. My baby boy tried to turn on the light, the predator had shut off the power. My princess, ran off to hide under the bed, as she always did when frightened. Not my boy. He began taking my tapes off I touched my head there was a thick white layer of cream smelled like bleach. I ran to the bathroom, looking for light, I found a lighter. I flick it and saw heavy cream with a terrible odor, I jumped in the shower, as I rinse, my hair fell out in patches and patches. I looked like I had cancer, I stayed in the shower hoping it was a dream. The morning came he didn't even care. He left for work like nothing happened. I called my job, and told them I was sick. I didn't send the kids to school. I stayed in the bathroom crying. I decided to end it all. I had no help. I bathed my kids, fed them, and kissed them. I decided to end my life. I remember telling my kids, 'I love you, and I am sorry I failed you' I kissed them and told them not to open the door. I went to the bathroom, and overdosed myself with pills. My boy had to use the bathroom real bad. He was smart. He knew I had a key in the hall. My baby boy managed to open the door, and saw me laying there dying. He ran to the hall and managed to see the super of the building they called 911 and saved me. My kids stayed with my friend.

I was in the hospital a month in a half, I learned skills and way to get help. When I got discharged I kept my kids at the friend's house. I then talked to my landlord, and told him to make a fake eviction and have him removed out the premises. My landlord did it, and he also faked a Marshall to serve him, he gave me my $2,000 deposit back on the spot. I didn't take anything with me, just my clothes and documents. I told my landlord to donate all my things. I wanted no memory of it, I got a restraining order, and I moved out of town. I'll admit it was hard as I started building my life. I got a storage and decided to buy things little by little. I slept in my car for a month with my kids. I remember I would bring them early morning to the storage and then to McDonalds where I would hold the door while they brush their teeth and they loved a good breakfast. I would work at a home making part time hours so I could be with my kids all the time.

I was able to grab control of my life. I was so worried about who can help silly me. I realized I could have done it all myself, and I did. I found resources, and I talked to a special person, Dr Allen who gave me the tools. That man that I once loved beat me severely, cut me, broke my tailbone, burned my hair off, strangled me, and mistreated his kids. It took courage to get away, no one understood why I stayed.

I never had any support, no tools, no hand to reach too. I thought at the time that was what I needed to leave, but it wasn't. I made a plan and I broke free. No more abuse. Physically, mentally, or emotionally. I became a counselor for battered woman found research, went to groups for therapy got my gun permit, moved out of state, took some self defense courses, and I say never again will ever be beaten by a man. Prepare a plan. Tell someone you love what you're going through, keep an emergency bag ready, put a set of keys outside your house, keep a phone close by, it doesn't have to be activated keep it charged because you can still dial 911 from it. Keep a journal at a family or friends house.

To all those that don't understand domestic violence, it's not easy leaving a bad relationship at times there's no support or they're afraid that love ones can get hurt. So many things can go wrong. You have to plan it. Make sure you're going to be safe. I learned one thing as a counselor you can tell them to leave, but you have to help them get tools so they can be safe. I have been free 11 years, and I thank God every day. I did it all on my own, I left and I outsmarted my abuser. He said I was dumb, but his words only defined me as long as I let him. I know better now.

✤ **Survivor: Marybel Carmona**

✳ ✳ ✳

I was in a relationship with a woman in 1994. She beat me and hit me with a full can of coke and even smashed a bottle of beer over my head resulting in 10 stitches. I loved her and every time she did it she said she was sorry, and that if I didn't act a certain way, it would never have happened. That she would never do it again.

This repeated itself till one evening , five days after she had given birth we were arguing because I had been out down to the local recycling center, and she thought I had been seeing other women. She picked up a leg from a broken table and smashed it round my face. I lost two teeth, she then kept hitting me on my back and head, and she smashed the fish tank. She picked up our daughter while she was in the stroller and literally threw her stroller with our daughter in it, into the front garden. I ran out and picked my daughter out of the stroller and ran. From that moment on I escaped, And never had to see her again thank God.

My second relationship that my partner was violent to me was in 2005. It started shortly, I would say about three months after we got together. She believed that if I was on the phone, I must be texting another woman. She started an argument one day and I let her see my phone. I had girls that were my friends nothing else on there. She told me I had to delete their numbers, and have nothing to do with them, which I did.

From that point on she had control. She told me one day out of the blue to prove I love her. I said how? She said get down on your hands and knees and beg me to stay with you. I said, but I am with you already and she said, you won't be if you don't do it. I did it.

I endured countless moments of humiliation. Then when we was about 5 months into the relationship she hit me in the face with her clenched fist. I don't know why she would have these outbursts.

I was so scared of what I would say when she got up in the morning, and what I'd say through the day, in fear of upsetting her. There was one night where I awoke with her slapping me in the face saying she hates me. I endured her hitting me whenever she wanted and even telling me I cannot have a cell phone or speak on anyone else's for over two years. She used to beat me with her keys in her clenched hand and everything. She told me I wasn't allowed to look into the road when I was with her as a passenger in a work van, so I had to keep my eyes down looking at me feet the whole way home. She beat me and gave me a black eye one day because she thought she saw me use my work colleagues phone as we drove off. I wasn't allowed to smoke or she would be finished with me, even though I smoked when I met her.

In the end I found out she was having an affair for over 18 months with one of my work colleagues. I ended up with our son and countless times she beat me in front of him. In the end I told social services, and the police but nothing happened. I gave our son back in 2009 and I do not see either of them now. She said if I go near him she will hurt him. I believe her. But as long as I stay away he is safe.

In 2009, around August, I met another woman. She told me she used to date women, but she said she wanted to be with me. I got with her and she was amazing at first. She was everything I wanted from someone. That changed after a couple of months. She got angry a lot, and I couldn't understand why. Then one day I met her ex and she said that she had always been like that and, very violent. She was on probation for beating her Ex girlfriend. I went home and confronted her about it,. She said she was on probation for assault on her Ex girlfriend.

She got pregnant and she got violent towards me one day when I said our relationship is over because she would get aggressive and controlling. She refused to understand that it was over, and every time she asked me to stay with her I said no. She wouldn't take no for an answer . She locked me in my own sitting room by standing by the door. Then she punched me so hard on the face it actually broke my cheekbone by the eye socket. I did go down and it hurt. But she was able to do this because I point blank, at the time, refused to even touch a woman physically not even to protect myself would I hit a woman or push her away. I tried to get to the front window to jump out and she jumped on my back and drew me to the bed in front of the window. The force of her doing this ripped open my hand as the handle catch snapped. She then put her hands round my throat and squeezed. I had given up all hope at this point, and I saw black spots then darkness.

She had strangled me with that much force it she broke five of her fingernails into my neck embedding them in there. When I awoke she was next to me asking me to forgive her and she was sorry. I said no and went to walk out. She hit me again. I managed to get the door open and ran out the front door. She had a knife from the kitchen and wanted to stab me. Our son was in the room the whole time. I phoned the police and they charged her with actual bodily harm. She admitted the charge. We got back together as she was bailed to my address. The police did not even ask me if I wanted her there, as she was not in the tenancy. I got beaten again a few months later and she was charged again. And then the final straw was when she chased me with a knife and I ran out of the flat. A while later she text me over 100 times in 20 minutes to get back with her she loved me, and shortly after all those texts, I get a text: "Your sitting room is on fire" .

I went to the flat and she had set fire to it. She was arrested and pleaded guilty in crown court to four accounts of actual bodily harm on me and arson of my flat. She got 16 weeks custody and was out in 8 weeks. She then threatened to hunt me down and slice my throat. I had enough and left my home town and never looked back. She has managed to get my number over and over and has tried ringing me. She texts me her undying love for me to this day, and still I ignore her. She messages me love messages on FB and I ignore her. But even after Four years have passed she still will not stop. And there is nothing I can do as the police said they are not threats of violence. I am 46 years old now. I am medium build and have muscles and very tall. Yet I would never ever lay my hand on a woman's head not even now. .

♛ **Survivor: Malcolm Robins**

* * *

My abuse started a very young age.... I was 5 years old. My friend at the time, her step father, used to molest her. One night I was sleeping over with her, and he did it to me. My parents were both physically and emotionally abusive. For as long as I can remember I was pushed down stairs held out a 2nd story window, tables were flipped over at me, and things thrown at me. At about 15 years old, I developed an eating disorder, due to years of emotional abuse from my mom. At 18, I was rapped by a stranger the weekend of my birthday. I told my boyfriend at the time he beat me up, and called me a liar, a slut, and knocked me unconscious.

After telling him that, the abuse continued, and got worse. I would be locked in the apartment unable to go to school, or work. He took my phone and car with him so I couldn't call anyone. He would drag me across the apartment and beat me till I would smoke weed with him.

After leaving him, I was with another man. He didn't beat me, instead he made me, one day smoke crack with him. He lied and told me it was weed. I had no idea. I came home from work one day looking for my dog. I was told by him, that the dog was next door. I went to get him, and was almost rapped by the neighbor. my dog jumped at him and saved me. I later found out, that my boyfriend sold me to the dealer.

The next boyfriend I had, went to jail, and asked a friend of his to look out for me while he was away. That 'friend', along with one of his friends, took turns raping me at a party one night. I told my mother, and she just said I was just looking for attention.

I had many other Girlfriends and Boyfriends after, who continued to abuse me in one way or another. One even pushed me down flights of steps several times. On one of these occasions my son almost went down with me, car seat and all, By the grace of God, he didn't. It ended there. I had been fighting my whole life, and I refused to do it anymore.

I didn't let my years of abuse cripple me. I started facing my demons, and I have forgiven my abusers. Don't let your abuse become your crutch, it does have a partial effect on who you are, but it doesn't define you. I have been free of abuse for four years. I AM survivor of domestic violence.

♛ **Survivor: Chris C.**

* * *

In 2004 I met my ex-husband in the UK (he is white South African). I am British and we dated for a little while and lived together. When he told me that he was coming back to South Africa to live, he asked me to come and move to South Africa with him. At this point he was a completely different person, very nice to me and not abusive at all. Up to this point I have never been a victim of domestic violence or abuse before. Like a lot of women I never thought such things would happen to me. In fact I hear this story a lot that when you are first with your boyfriend or husband they always start off being non abusive and nice, the same thing for me. Then later on the abuse starts.

No one ever deserves violence and there are many reasons why a woman doesn't leave. In my case I am in the most abusive country on earth, where it is always legal to abuse women, In fact South African men are the most abusive men in the world. Women have so few little rights and generally go with the attitude that abuse is always normal and so legal. It is impossible to press charges against men over assault or domestic violence. South Africa has the highest statistics - 1 woman in this country is killed by an abusive partner/spouse every 6 hours. It also has the highest level of rape of about 1400 women are raped in this country every day. What makes it worse even after a highly publicized case of Oscar Pretorius for murdering his girlfriend - they will never overturn the law to protect women. I am also a lawyer but am not legally allowed to work over here as a foreign national.

Very early on after moving to this country my ex-husband starts becoming emotionally abusive and financially controlling. About a year after this - he started becoming physically abusive with me. Needless to say it destroyed me and devastated me. I would fight back in the beginning as I am not the sort of person to be punched and kicked but he was stronger than me and would get angrier for this and would often dislocate my left arm and kick my bad left leg back that I would be on the floor in screaming pain and would be kicked and punched more. I would often be covered in bruises and injuries. He would often punch and kick me all over, dig his nails into my skin, pull my hair, smack my head against the wall and shake my body. Then there were times when he would throw heavy groceries at me and slam a door in my face on purpose. The first time I went to the police about his physical violence they just laughed in my face and said "this is South Africa. Abuse is legal over here and you are a foreign national with a South African man and must put up with it. " I tried yet again in another state of KZN (the first time I went to the police was in Gauteng). Exactly the same story. By the time I became pregnant - I could no longer defend myself. I nearly miscarried my children as he would abuse physically when I was pregnant too.

You may ask why I stayed. Unfortunately after being in this country for a short time where I had no one and still don't, I had no money and no one could help me with the airfare to go home. The British Government wouldn't help me. I was stuck in a country where I am not legally allowed to work in and had no credit card. Had no form of money and my ex-husband was so controlling with money that he would never let me go home and still won't. All the time my ex would always emotionally abuse me too and tell me repeatedly what a terrible person I was and how I deserved no better. My attitude always was that I don't. He constantly criticized me about everything under the sun. I think if I hadn't been such a strong person and knew other people who knew I am a good person with bad circumstance and had belief in myself and have kids, I'm not sure I would have survived it. It was only after I asked for a divorce repeatedly that he finally relented and agreed for us to get divorced.

We separated in January 2014 and no longer live together. I think if I also didn't have kids if I would have survived it. I always held onto the belief too that I did not deserve any of this and it's a basic human right to not be abused. And that I deserved better, especially with cancer, I deserved a better life. I now have just that, a better life.

♛ **Survivor: Anoushka Santinelli**

* * *

I met my Ex-husband at a convenience store late one night in September 1977. We were both 21 years old. He was tall, very good looking, had a smile that could light up a room, and the attraction was instant for both of us. I returned to the same store every night for a week or so before he finally asked me out. We dated for three months and decided to get married.

We married in December 1977 and moved into our first apartment. We lived in the same building as my sister and as we were very close, I naturally told her everything. The first time he hit me was because I had talked to my sister about how moody he seemed to be and I was concerned. Apparently I was not supposed to talk to her about things like this, even though he also refused to answer my repeated questions about what was wrong. I was told to stay away from her. I, of course, didn't listen. This was my sister.

I waited until after he went to work one morning and walked over to her apartment. I was there just a few minutes. I had taken a pregnancy test and it was positive and I wanted to share the news. I walked back to our apartment and he was back and waiting for me. He was angry when I told him where I had been. I was not afraid, I didn't know I was supposed to be. He slapped me. I was in total shock. He then proceeded to pick me up and toss me against the bedroom wall. I was kicked and hit repeatedly until he stopped abruptly and left for work. I cleaned up and calmed my small son (I had had him out of wedlock before we met) and locked my doors.

I stayed in the apartment all day. He came home like nothing happened and all was quiet. I was confused and not sure what to do. I went to work the next day after passing a long night of cramps and small back pain. I miscarried my baby at work. I was devastated. I don't remember if I had ever told him about the baby or not. I remember lying down in the nurse's lounge and spending most of the day there. There were no more incidents for quite a while. I thought maybe it was just a time when he was upset or angry over something, and things would be okay again soon.

We moved into a small two bedroom house next door to his best friend and his wife. We started going out more and life was better. Then came the night he came home angry over something that happened at work. I tried to talk to him and calm him down, but he beat me pretty good for the second time. I ran out the door into the front yard, but he followed me and proceeded to kick me and call me names. It stopped when his friend stopped him. I managed to get into the house and once again nurse my wounds.

The beatings got more frequent after that. He would get angry over small things like his clothes not being washed or not enough ice in his tea, or dinner not being ready the way he liked it. Sometimes, I was beat and never knew why. I had quit my job at the nursing home, and started working as a desk clerk at a local hotel and an apartment was included in with my salary. We moved onto the property which was closer to his work place also. He started staying home more and missing work. We were getting more in debt since he wasn't working very much. Our car was starting to need a lot of work plus with me working the midnight shift, we now had daycare expenses for my son.

We often fought over money, and his staying at home to watch TV and sleep. Some of the fights were bad, some were just arguments. There were times I went to work with red marks on my neck or face. I tried to hide them with makeup. I dared not tell my family because he had threatened them, and I wanted to protect everyone if I could. I had male friends from school who offered to take care of things, but I refused the help. After seeing my condition, some of the hotel's regular customers took up a collection for me so I could leave. I was scared and appreciated the money. I hid it and started trying to figure out how to leave. My problem was I loved this man. He didn't drink and when he wasn't angry, he was so sweet and he had always been good to my son. The baby never saw him angry or hitting me. I thank God all the time for that blessing.

The police had been called several times to aid me, but since I had fought back, he could also have pressed charges against me. Times did not favor a battered wife and there were no laws to protect me. I was on my own. Most of the officers that came to our home were his pals from the reserve unit he was in. I felt alone and could see no immediate way out. So I suffered in silence, except for what I related to my sister. She suffered right along with me. I had tried to leave at one point and she came over to help me gather up some stuff since my car was not starting. He walked in and he hit both of us. She was a tomboy and gave it all she got. I managed to get her to leave without me. I wanted her safe. After that, I started, in earnest, planning my escape. I had reached the point I was afraid he would kill me. He had threatened it several times and now it was getting really bad. There was the time I had car trouble and a police officer followed me home and I was beaten after he left for allowing him to follow me home. There was the stalking I endured while at work or with family. There were the beatings that took place if I talked to someone I wasn't supposed to whether I knew they were off limits or not. It was my fault, always.

On the night I left, I had spent the day putting clothes, and baby things into my car. I cooked dinner as usual, took care of the baby as usual and waited. He came home in a bad mood. I got slapped for the lack of ice in his tea, even though the tea was hot, he didn't even consider that. I waited. I just had to pull off one last bravado though. While he watched TV, I fixed a pot of grits. He often slept in the nude under a sheet. I plotted and waited. He finally dozed off about midnight or so. I picked up the baby and put him in the car. I had the car parked outside the front door and running. I went in and got my pot of grits and calmly walked over to the bed and poured them on him. Of course, reflecting back on it now, I could have been long gone before he woke up if I hadn't wanted to have a final word. But, I just had to have one final move. He jumped up screaming and I was running for my life. He got to the car just as I put it into gear after locking the door. I was crying and shaking. He reached through the window and grabbed a handful of my hair and I floored the gas. I drove to my sister's home and she was shocked to see me. My brother in law slept in the living room that night to make sure there was not trouble.

I didn't sleep very much, I was too nervous. I went to my parents home the next day and he didn't contact me till the third day. He called and wanted to know when I was coming home. I was incredulous. How could he even think I would go back. My brother was still living at home at the time, and he made sure he would be there most of the time to protect my family. But nothing ever happened.

I filed for divorce after a year of separation and he never showed up or contacted me again. That was in the summer of 1980. We didn't even make it a year. When I left that night, I never looked back. I did hear from him in January 2005. I had my youngest son in the hospital with a collapsed lung and my children were calling on a regular basis for updates. I was shocked when my older son called to tell me he had heard from my Ex by accident. My son worked for AOL at the time and my ex had called for help with his account. He caught on the my son's last name was the same as his. He made the connection. He wanted to talk to me. I was curious and consented. When the call came in, I was shaking and nervous. After some small talk, he said he was sorry for what he put me through and he didn't know why he had done it. He was not that kind of a person and he wanted my forgiveness. I gave it to him. I was never one to hold grudges.

We spoke again off and on for a few months after that and then I lost touch again. I have since moved back to my hometown and through the wonder of Facebook, he has found me again. We talked and he once again asked for my forgiveness and asked me out for dinner. We talked about what had happened and why. He said he won't bother me and just wants to find a way to make it up to me. He has met my other children. It was only right since my next to the oldest son bears his name. I was pregnant when I finally filed for my divorce and I made sure he never knew. It wasn't his, but by law, I had to give him his surname. So he wanted to meet that son. My children and son in law were on guard, but the visit went off without a hitch. That was over 2 months ago. I have only heard from him again once. He is divorced and alone, so am I. But I am happy to be alone. I have no thoughts of reconciling with him. I have told him so. Our history is too painful. I still care for him, but that is not a bridge I want to cross again. I know I should have left after he hit me the first time, but I was young and in love. I didn't know about the pattern of abuse until it became a national movement.

I can think back and see it all so clearly, the controlling, the isolation from family and friends, and all of the other signs. They were clearly there. I am thankful I escaped with my life and no permanent damage and that my son has no memory of those times. I have been married 2 times since then and both marriages had a degree of abuse. I have been through mental and emotional abuse and almost accepted it, just to not be alone again. But after my third husband left, I mourned and I am grateful and happy being alone. I have no fear of going home and opening my door. I have the joy of my children, grandchildren and family to keep me company. It is very liberating. If I could help just one person escape the hell I was subjected to, it would have made my hell worth it. When my brother in law hit my sister a couple of years ago, I wasn't here to help her in person, but when she called me, I was able to help her open her eyes and get help. Thankfully, he hasn't done it again and he returned to his spiritual roots and they are still together. I only wanted to be loved and cherished and to grow old with someone at my side. But this is infinitely better than being afraid of someone who is supposed to love me.

Survivor: Carol T.

* * *

It seems from the time I was a little girl and meaningless, perverts seemed to find me wherever I went. Let me start by saying my parents divorced when I was 8 years old. My brother & I stayed with my mom. I don't know why but seemed like the best thing to do at the time. From the very beginning my brother and I were treated like "we were in the way" so to speak. Made to stay outside all day. Of we wanted something to drink. We used the water hose. She kept us locked out. Till it got dark. But before we were put outside we had daily chores. Sweep, mop, vacuum, dust, wash dishes and cook meals. From the time I could pull a chair up to stove or sink. I cooked. Back in my early years I used a lot of Campbell's soup. As we got older it got worse. My mom was in bed all day every day. For as long as I can remember I cooked and cleaned for her. I got up got me and my brother off to school. When I came home I'd cook supper or whatever meal. Fixed a tray with plates of food, something to drink and whatever else was needed for the meal. And carried it to her bed. The pressure to be perfect and try to out think her to keep her from being mad at me for something, Was unbearable at times. If we did something that didn't please her. We were beat. Our home life was hell.

Somewhere around 1970 my mom was dating a guy. Which we liked. We all went to a tab boil party at his family home. I was about 8. Most of the kids were all down at the neighbors house, so I went down there too. I saw a man walking down the hot road, shorts, no shirt or shoes. He lived at the house I had just left. Well how in the world did this creep pick me out to be so gullible? I still don't know. I was always trying to please and help anyone. So when this old man asked me would I help him make a phone call. I said sure .

He shows me to a back bedroom. While I'm heading over to pick up the phone. I hear the door lock. He grabs the phone from me. Shoves me on the bed with his weight on me and the smell of beer reeks from him. He takes off my underwear and his shorts. And tells me " I'm fixing to show you what your mom likes to do". I can't scream, I'm too scared. As he tries to enter me. Some kid beats on the window and says something. Which makes him jump up. I ran back to where my mom was. But I never told her what happened. I was afraid I'd get in trouble.

Soon after that my mom's best friends husband molested me while he thought my brother and I, were asleep. I laid there crying smelling his beer breath and my baby brother saw it too. They were our next door neighbors. Never told my mom about that either until the day I turned 18. She cried and wondered why I never told her? The first man had died by then. But the man that molested me, I found out some years later. Had written a book about how to keep kids safe from predators. Funny because I wonder if it was it guilt, or if I was a test subject? I don't know. I was about 11 when he molested me.

Some time in between those 2 events. My own grandpa was going to do something to me. What I don't know. Because he heard my grandma drive up. He laid me on his bed in his room. He took off my pants. And pulled down his khaki pants with his paisley boxers. Thank goodness she drove up. I never told her either. I couldn't. After so many things had happened. I figured it was me. Something I was doing wrong. I have been through so much hell in my life. When I write this all down. I can't even believe it.

As the years went on my home life got worse. I was my mom's slave, and she was a cruel and relentless slave master. She controlled everything I did or wanted to do. When I got old enough to graduate. I married my high school sweetheart. After he shot his self in front of me because I had broken up with him. So I took him back for fear he would kill himself, and I would be to blame.

We married in October of 1980. Had my son in September 1981. His parents had to drag him out of a bar to make him come to hospital to see his only child. So we had hell. He lived in the bars while I lived at home with his family. His dad would go out many nights to look for him. He never believed that was his son. Not till years later. Went for my 6 weeks check up and the doctors told me I had a venereal disease. I cried and cried. I had to stay and sit in a room, after I took a huge dose of antibiotics. I was suppose to tell my husband. Did I? Hell no! I wanted his penis to fall off and hurt like hell. That day after I got the results. I packed my things and moved back in with my mom, and the hell she delivered.

At that time I wanted to go to school, and back then they paid you to go to trade school. I had put in a few applications around town. The day I took my entrance exam to see where to be placed. I got home and some restaurant called and offered me a job. My mom would only help me with my child, and a way back and forth to work, if I took the waitress job. She didn't want me to better myself. So I forgot about school. Had no other choice. Every week when I got paid, I gave her every cent. Including my AFDC aid for dependent children. Because my husband never paid ordered child support. She said I owed her every penny for housing, food and rent of her car. I was so stuck. If I ever did get to go out with friends, I used my tip money to pay her to babysit her only grandchild.

I started dating this real nice guy. Came from a good family. Very good looking. His mom asked me to come work for her. She gave me a truck to drive. I was there from 7 am-7 pm 6 days a week. I made $75 a week. I was able to bring my son with me, because I kept kids, and ran errands for their hardware store. I also cleaned house and cooked daily. Most nights I stayed there with them, but I always took my mom a plate of food. On the nights I did go home, my mom would remove my light bulb, toilet tissue and tooth paste. I'd still give her $25 week. She said 'you don't pay for these items so you don't get to use them.' When I asked what was the $25 I paid her weekly for. Her answer was to hang my close in the closet. I could go on and on. But I won't.

That man later became my second husband. He seemed like a nice guy from a good family. His sister and I were best friends. We dated for several months. And started planning our wedding. I never saw the signs before we married, But it went downhill really fast. I would get slapped for looking at him wrong. I wore a plain white t-shirt once and got a severe beating. If I rearranged the furniture, changed the channel or when his sister took off her shoes and put them on the couch I got beat. I had to work or I wasn't allowed things for my son. I got pretty good at make-up over my bruises on my face. I was down to a size 5 and I'm 5-10 1/2. Couldn't eat or sleep. My son would be jumping in his back, trying to get him off if me many times. Once I didn't want to have sex and he started beating me. Shoved me between the bed and wall. Put on his boots and started kicking me and jumping up and down on my breasts. They were solid black. I remember standing in the shower crying from the pain. He said I made him do it, and told me to shut up.

The worst beating I took was for waiving at a friend while we were driving down the road. He threw thus big gulp coke all over me and my new Easter shirt. When he got out of the truck I locked the door. Thought I could stay safe. He sat in the porch screaming at me saying I was making a scene. I could tell he was getting worse so I opened the truck door he got me out of the truck. Threw me over his shoulder and threw me over a chair. And processed to beat me to death. I remember laying on the floor on my side and he hit me as hard as he could with his fist. When he did I couldn't breathe. I was scared to death. He said I was making it up while he drug me through broken glass in the kitchen. He hit me several more times in the face. All I can remember is putting my son out the bedroom window telling him to go next door and call my mom.

She took me to doctor the next day. I still couldn't breathe. I remember sitting on the X-ray table and the X-ray tech saying u must have been in a hell of a car wreck? I started crying and agreed. I had three cracked ribs, a collapsed left lung, a dislocated shoulder and a concussion. Needless to say, even after I reported it to police, He turned around and pressed charges on me. The DA here never did a thing about it.

After I healed, I went back. Yes, I know, stupid. This time he hurt my son. He was 4. And we had company over. And he must have did something to piss him off. I could hear him crying in the bedroom. Not thinking he was doing anything inappropriate. When they came down the hall he swatted his bottom and said 'Don't you run to your Mama. Sit your ass on the couch'. He went back outside with our company. Well in a few minutes my son came In the kitchen by the stove where I was cooking. And said 'mommy I got something in my foot' I said 'ok lay back let me see'. As he tried to lay down on the white floor he screamed! I looked at his back and was in horror. He had bloody cuts from his shoulders down to his knees. Oh my God! It was awful! I sent him out the front door while I distracted him. I said 'What the hell did you use to whip him?' He bragged while pulling up his pants and said 'I used a wire clothes hanger and there ain't shit you going to do about it.' Well that was it. I was done. I could take the beating. But not my child!

 **Survivor: Anonymous**

* * *

It began in my junior year of high school. I had been going to an alternative learning center as an extension of the mainstream high school. As this option suited me best at that time in my life. I had a lot of instability in my home life. My mother had been a nurse, a job that she was amazing at performing. However she also had been diagnosed with bipolar and manic depressive disorders. So her ability to maintain consistent work hours was seldom and occasional at best. My whole life has memories of her in and out of psychiatric hospitals. When she was unable to work during times, it was a very dark time for me.

I am an only child in my family, and my father was usually an absentee parent. Not because of choice, but because he was a hard working man who tried his best at supporting his family in the best way he knew how at the time. He had 2-3 jobs he worked simultaneously at any given time in my life. That made him rarely witness to the trauma and distress I felt on most days at home alone with my mother. When he was around I did not want to discuss the abuse. I simply wanted to be happy and safe with my dad. Those times brought me great comfort. At the same time it made me feel that I had to deal with these horrific events on my own. That this was "normal" routine for everybody.

The day I met Johnnie was a day I will not soon forget. He was the class clown. He was tall, dark, and handsome. He had a comforting sense about his presence. When he first approached me, I thought to myself "Why is this popular guy who can get any other girl interested in me?" I felt beautiful, wanted, and protected as we started dating. He told me what I wanted to hear. As I look back, I allowed him to tell me those things. I longed for that type of connection. That was my first of many mistakes. I gave him that power over me.

The first year that we dated he had moved into the home I shared with my dad. By then my mother had moved out. During that time we both mutually worked full time jobs and in school. But going into our senior year in high school he committed his first of several felonies in our seven year relationship. He had committed a fraud at his sales job that resulted in the charges and convictions of: Identification Theft Felony and Fraud, Felony. My dad told me that I needed to consider breaking up, and moving on. But didn't want to "abandon" him. I felt that I could "help him change". This was my second mistake. Not long after that time was when the cheating rumors and hints started showing up. But I refused to acknowledge or accept those possibilities. We moved to Atlanta, Georgia to try our go at a life together and start fresh. While there he had talked me into becoming an exotic dancer to support us, and as he would tell me is just until he can find work.. Well what was supposed to only be temporary work turned into more than 18 months. of dancing. To feed his alcohol, drug sales, and careless spending nights out with his guy friends.

He left me in Georgia going into our third year together to go to his court dates for the felony charges. Since I was alone I had no protective male presence around me. A customer of my club had noticed, followed me back to the motel I was staying at alone. He raped and beat me right behind the dumpster by the soda machine. After cops had told me that I brought that trauma upon myself because of what I did for a job. I got a Greyhound bus ticket as soon as it became available out of there. I only grabbed what I could carry of personal belongings out of my very first car I had worked very hard to buy myself, and left it behind. It had two flat tires and engine problems, and by then that I knew would not make it, driving all the way back. This was very emotional for me as I felt like I had left a piece of my life and who I was behind. I felt abandoned myself by him. When I got back to my home state I had entered into a battered women's shelter as I didn't have anywhere else to go at that time. During my time there I had found out I was pregnant. I feared that it may have been my rapist's child. Thankfully I later found out that my son wasn't a product of that assault. He is an exact duplicate of his father.

    We got back together and gotten an apartment together midway through that pregnancy. At which time the physical abuse had started becoming more consistent and more volatile. I had gone into preterm labor multiple times as a result. I had hoped that when our son was born that he would realize that he was making a mistake and decide, or be willing to, be a better man and father. But that was a short lived hope. I had our second son 18mos later. He had lost the job he had around same time. So I had little option other than to join the military, leaving him to be the primary caregiver for our sons. I had an irrational belief that even though he abused me, that he would never harm them or put them in harm's way. But four months into my service, I had become aware that my once healthy two year old had been in the hospital for pneumonia resulting in him needing to have chest tubes in his right lung. I had soon after been discharged on a Family Hardship-Honorable conditions. When I returned home my bank account was nearly a thousand dollars in negative balance. He had had full access to my income while I was away. I had been receiving $1,600 on the 1st and the 15th of every month over a six month period of time. His only responsibility was to maintain our car, and feed/clothe our sons. He was living with his mother at time to save while I was away, then when I returned from training we could then purchase a house. It didn't go that way at all. In fact, two months after I had returned we had started living in family shelters downtown. This is where things took a drastic turn for the worst.

    We had gone to some old friends' house we had known since our school days to catch up. He had been drinking a lot. An argument erupted as we were leaving with our children. He smashed my head into the windshield of our car on passenger side as I stood outside of vehicle. That caused the windshield to crack and leave an imprint of my head. I still remember the sound my skull made as it cracked with the impact. I don't remember much immediately following that. But I do remember when we arrived to the shelter and parked across street in public parking lot, I told him to go ahead in while I cleaned my face before going in. It was close to curfew at the shelter and I wanted to make sure that we had a place to sleep for the night. I was not thinking about myself. I wasn't thinking clearly. I was in shock.

When I was alone outside walking towards shelter I had been hit in the head from behind knocking me unconscious. I awoke to a man taping my arms behind my back, pants removed and tape over my mouth. I remember as the man raped me I had seen a car resembling the make and model of our same car not far away. But I had been hurt so badly on my head that I couldn't process what was happening. When the man left I was barely conscious enough to hear car driving off. After laying there for I'm not sure how long, I woke up and tried to undo the tape by rubbing my wrists on broken shards of glass in the alley he left me in. Once freed, I pulled my pants on and walked the 8 blocks to a gas station to ask for help. A city police officer was there. He took my statement, brought me to hospital, they perform a rape-kit exam, did a head x-ray and ct test. I had two skull fractures, a concussion, my lip was badly cut from the windshield, and both eyes were almost swollen shut, but I was released next morning. I went back to the shelter where we had been staying and was immediately embraced by my husband. I don't know why, but I was comforted by his apologies for the night before and his concern for where I had been all night. I told him about rape, he seemed genuinely concerned and surprised in his reaction. So when I met with detective several days later at his office, I was in paralyzing shock when he told me the DNA from the rape kit came back as Johnnie's. I couldn't emotionally accept that he had the potential to hurt me to that extent. So I had walked out of that detective's office without ever pressing charges or going back.

I look back now and realize how bad this sounds and looks from the outside looking in on this story. But I ask you to understand that abuse had been all I had known my whole life. I didn't have the coping skills or self esteem needed to overcome my want and desire for this marriage to work. So when the verbal and physical abuse began with him, I felt like if I could just tough it out, that things would eventually get better. I also irrationally thought that he was simply expressing his stress at that time just in whatever way he could express it. My mother had told me during most of this relationship that I would fail as a wife, that our marriage was doomed anyways. I was determined to prove her wrong.

When we moved into our last apartment together, I contemplated a lot over our marriage and the life we have had over these few years. I decided very rapidly and carefully coming up with a goal to get both of my sons and myself out as soon as I could. I think he had sensed it, because he started keeping one or the other with him at all times. Or we had went to destinations as a family unit. Leaving me little opportunity to make solid resources known, or put plans into place. Thwarting any attempt I made.

On December 23rd, 2007 is the night I almost lost my life. We had neighbor who lived above us come down to our place to play cards, or dominoes with us, he had brought his girlfriend with him. Johnnie had opened a large half gallon bottle of vodka and started making the games more of a drinking game for them. I refused to drink when he did, as he made me too nervous to enjoy myself anyway. He didn't know how to stop once he started. After about an hour and a half and little over half of this bottle gone, he almost seemed to flip a switch. Asking the neighbor and his girl to leave and that we were going to bed. I knew something was up, he had the look in his eyes that was my clue to be on guard when the door closed.

When he turned back around he punched my square center of my nose, I heard the bone crack under his knuckles. He then started accusing me of blatantly flirting with the male neighbor, right in front of him. I told him that I would never do that. That the liquor is just clouding his mind and that we should just go to bed and discuss this tomorrow. I then tried to walk away hoping that he would be receptive to the idea. I was tragically wrong. The beating ensued with him grabbing me by back of neck and hair and him wrapping my waist length hair around one fist several times making it impossible to pull away. I had been tossed and dragged all through that apartment. He broke my nose, jaw, four ribs, dislocated my right knee, three more skull fractures. Then he dragged me to our bedroom putting me on our bed, climbing on top straddling me, and pursued strangling me. As the vision began tunneling and extremities began weakening, I started hearing my dad's voice inside me telling me 'You better not let this SOB take you out....I taught you better than that... don't leave me and those boys of yours... come on fight!'

As I opened my eyes again I saw in the doorway of our room, was our 2 &1/2 year old son watching this happen. Our son was watching his father killing his mother. How did it get this far? What have I done? Is this the life and legacy I'm leaving them? I mustered up whatever strength I had in me, and using the only leg I have left I reared up kneeing Johnnie right where it counts, knocking the wind out of him. I pushed him off and weakly attempted to grab our son and getting up the stairs to neighbor. I'm pounding on door pleading for help, I hear him approaching, screaming my name in such rage it made my blood chill to ice. The neighbor opens door in disbelief as to what was in front of him. I was draining blood out of my broken nose, jaw hanging at an odd angle caused by fracture and my badly injured leg's knee cap had been pushed to the outside part of my leg. And blood everywhere on my body. I must've looked horrific to him. Thankfully he pulled my son and I in his door just as Johnnie was reaching top of stairway. As he shielded us from Johnnie, my son hid in the bedroom with neighbor's girlfriend, as I had began making my way to back stairs to get our other son who was still in our apartment. I had to go get him, I had nothing else on my mind at that moment other than my need to get and protect him. I grabbed my cell phone on the way back out of door with our son in my arms. As I made the 911 call I heard him coming down the same back stairway I was trying to climb. I still remember the deafening thud his body made as I locked door of our apartment. Our neighbor came in the front door in a hurry to assist me in any way he could. This repeated back and forth continued a as Johnnie kept trying to find a way in to the apartment. All the while screaming " I'm going to kill you bitch!!... You hear me?!?... You will never be safe..." By the time cops arrived he had disappeared. This led to a cat-mouse type of event as cops left looking for him, not locating him, me calling back, then returning, failing to find him several times.

During my final call for help Johnnie had breached the door and gained possession of a butcher knife. repeatedly attempting to lunge at me in any way he could, While neighbor stood between me and Johnnie. While call was in progress he grabbed cell from my hands and snapped phone in half ending my call for help. As cops arrived Johnnie was escaping out the back door.

This whole time I knew Johnnie had been without shoes on, and being December and ice/snow being outside I told cops he couldn't have gone far. Told them to check the basement door in back stairway that led to building's laundry room. The ordeal ended with the police at gunpoint took him into custody. I had been told later that night by hospital physician that had he squeezed any longer on my neck he would've crushed my esophagus. The bruises were so bad you could almost make out fingerprints.

I spent the next few months trying to hide and disappear from him. In and out of court. I had pleaded with the judge in his chambers surrounded by defense, D.A., advocate, to not give him a plea agreement. That it would endanger sons and myself. The judge gave him a deal anyways, Johnnie only had to spend six months in custody. Six months!! Upon his release I was supposed to be contacted by an automated phone message system that the state provided for victims of a crime informing them when the inmate is being released. It is supposed to give the victim time to get in safe location before the release. Upon his release he was not to make contact with any of us. He got right on bus and went to that very apartment we had been sharing. I was gone but not far, because I had only moved few miles away. Continuing my rental arrangement with management of properties.

He had stalked and found me not long after. Kidnapping me from bus stop I was at. Johnnie & his best friend took me to an abandoned house. They raped me repeatedly over a 12 hour period. Between bathing me in bleach baths, beating me, and assaulting me, my own mother in-law would come in and overlook the whole ordeal and ask me "if it hurt", then walking out. They later dumped me on side of road in residential area, cops found me as they passed by. Took me to hospital, of course the staff wanted a rape exam. I had refused. Why? Because I didn't want to be raped yet again by some piece of metal or plastic when i had already been violated. I couldn't handle anymore. I knew who did it. I felt I didn't need to have the tests when I could give statement telling the police I knew the perpetrators. Well, I lost that guarantee when the charges were, a short time later, dropped.

I took my boys with me on the soonest bus we could book out of state. It was our only option of survival. I had gained the assistance of an advocacy program in the town I moved to. They then helped me get legal assistance in pursuing a divorce and termination of his parental rights. The judge here was of no mercy in my attempts. Johnnie had appeared at this court date claiming he was representing himself. Which led to the judge allowing this man to interrogate, badger, and belittle me on the stand, attempting to shred my character. The judge decided to give Johnnie supervised visitations that would be held at the advocacy building only a county away from us, and child support payments for both kids at $264/mo. Johnnie was told he would have to do an intake process for the visitations before he could start seeing the boys. He never showed up to do that intake.

That court date occurred in '09. He has paid $88 total since this started. He is well over $14,000 in arrearage. He has not faced one day in jail for failure to pay. I am also told by the Attorney General office here that it is MY responsibility, NOT theirs, to locate his current information, and provide them with that so they can "enforce the court orders". By doing this I have provided them with all documents that prove I would be endangering us in the process. Leaving me to decide whether the money, if received, is worth the risk. What I have learned through this whole process is that we desperately need changes in these laws. Survivors like myself need the help of the government to make it easier and possible to escape. Completely escape. Safely. This lack of accountability is maddening to me. During the time we have been free of his wrath, I have gained my voice back. My sons have adjusted very well. With the help of my dad, who lives with us, and new friends here I have recovered from the immediate trauma. But I still struggle daily with PTSD. Recently I had been contacted by a woman who gave me a HOPE I had long thought had been expunged by his torment and ghost. I want to scream from the senate steps that this needs to stop!

I will find my way. I have no idea yet exactly how I will do that, But I will not stop until I do. I have learned that I don't and won't ever have to tolerate being treated that way by any other man. My sons have their Mama here. They don't feel unsafe. They have succeeded very well in school. That is proof that I'm giving them what they need. That makes my heart have peace and comfort, knowing that I have been able to give them something better. To give them the chance not to feel what I had my whole life. They are my legacy, and my primary purpose, is to raise them into strong, hard working, high morale, young men that I release out into the world when the time is right. Men like their father never could, or would be. If I can make that happen, I have done what I'm meant to do. Please be kind to yourself.

Survivor: E. Marie

* * *

  I first met the man who would become my abuser, and worst nightmare when we were twelve years old. We lived in the same neighborhood and had the same group of friends. When I first met him I thought he was the most gorgeous boy that I had ever seen and I was instantly drawn to his charming and outgoing personality. He was popular and friendly and very likeable. We spent virtually every single day together just hanging out and I considered him my best friend. He was always kind to me, would hold my hand when we walked anywhere and would protect me like a big brother. I had no way of knowing the demon that was inside, or that this would be the man would eventually lead me straight into the pits of hell.

  I didn't have the courage to tell him I liked him until we were nineteen. We started dating but his personality changed. He was always jealous and constantly worried that I was going to cheat on him. He would always make sure to announce to any man that were around us that I was his girlfriend. At first it would make me feel so special and loved. Clearly he wanted everyone to know I was his because he loved me. But I was wrong. It was only jealously. When we were around women he would never announce that I was his girlfriend, introduce me, or acknowledge my very existence. One day we went hiking with friends to some caves and we hit a spot that was very rocky and steep. His friend hiked down first and then turned around and offered his hand out to help me down. I took his hand, climbed down, and then released his hand. My boyfriend was all over me so fast I didn't even have time to think. Even though neither his friend nor I had done anything wrong, he completely ignored his friend for offering to help me down, and instead took all his rage out on me. He started screaming at me in front of everybody, called me a whore and a cheater, and 'HOW DARE I DO THAT!?' I didn't even know what I had done wrong…. I balled my eyes out all the way home. This wasn't the man that I had fallen in love with. Our relationship only lasted about three months. For how jealous and worried he was about me cheating, he eventually admitted that he had cheated on me and I dumped him. My heart was completely broken and I was depressed for a year. I never thought he would do that to me, especially when he was so concerned that I was going to cheat on him.

Eleven years pass. In those eleven years, I get married and then divorced. I had never stopped thinking about him and decided to seek him out. When I found him, he immediately showered me with affection and attention and everything I wanted to hear: "I have been looking everywhere for you, I am so happy you found me, I am so in love with you, you are my soul mate, I am so sorry I hurt you and will never cheat on you again, I want to marry you, I want to have a family with you, we can be happy…" We started dating again. He told me he was single and that he wanted to be with only me forever and that solid relationships are built on trust. I agree. Because he pushes the trust and honesty issue so heavily, I shared with him some of my deepest secrets. I told him of the affair I had during my marriage, I told him that I made the decision not to tell my husband about the affair because there was no point in hurting him further. He suspiciously has no secrets to share. At this point, we are living in different cities and things aren't adding up about who he lives with and why I can't come stay with him when I come to town. Things seem odd to me but I have no proof that anything is going on. Until one morning when I receive a text saying "call me as soon as you get this message." I called him and a woman answered the phone. Not only did she tell me that she was involved with him, but that there were two additional girlfriends as well, for a grand total of four women that he was currently seeing. None of us had known about each other. I confronted him with all the evidence and I dumped him again. I was devastated and confused. How do you tell someone you want to marry them when you have three other girlfriends??

A month or so passes and he messages me telling me he loves me, misses me and everything was a big misunderstanding. He tells me that I am, in fact, the one he wants to marry and have a family with, and the one he is IN LOVE with. He tells me that he is single and all of the other women are out of his life now, cause he never wanted them, he wanted me. He knows I am about to move to the city he is living in and he wants me to be with him. I make the decision to take him back one final time. I make it very clear to him that if he cheats on me again that I will never take him back again. I had no idea that the cheating was about to become the very least of my worries.

I move into the same city as him and he asks me to move in with him, and I tell him no. I get my own apartment on the other side of town. He becomes extremely upset with my decision to live alone. He begins coming over every single day and starts slowly bringing his belongings into my house. For awhile, I don't mind because I like spending time with him. Then things start to change.

He begins to exhibit extreme jealousy and constant concerns about where I am, and what I am doing. He starts to go through my phone and read EVERY single text message, email, piece of information he can find. He begins to quiz me on every single male friend I have. HAVE I FUCKED THAT GUY??? He friends my male friends on Facebook, people he has never even met in real life and if they don't accept his request then it means for sure that I have something going on with them. I try to keep the peace by allowing him to go through my phone whenever he wants to prove to him I am being faithful. But it doesn't help to make anything better. My explanations never matter. The fact that I have male friends means that I am a raging whore.

He becomes so angry with me that he starts punching holes in the walls. I tell him he needs to leave, that I am done, that nobody should live this way. He pushed me down on the bed and pinned me there so I couldn't move. Then he tells me he loves me and asks me to marry him. I tell him to fuck off and get out of my house. He says he doesn't have to leave because his belongings have been in my home for over thirty days and I would have to get an eviction notice. He also tells me that if I leave him, he will make a phone call to my ex-husband and inform him of my affair. The tone of his voice chills me to the bone. I run out of the house and contact an attorney who tells me that is true. I would have to get an eviction notice. Even though he isn't on the lease and it is MY home! If I go ahead and get the eviction notice then he will know for sure that I am done and this will only anger him further, and worse, he isn't required to move out immediately. I am still trapped in the home with him or I leave him in my apartment with my belongings. Nor did I want him contacting my ex-husband. It isn't his place to make these decisions and ruin other people's lives further. What the heck was wrong with this man? I return home and don't know what to do. I hope for the best. Maybe things will get better?

For awhile things do get better. My lease is up at my apartment and we discuss moving to a new apartment together. My goal was mostly to get his name on the lease this time because I figured at a minimum he would stop punching holes in the walls. But it doesn't take long after moving into our new apartment for things to get really bad. We are constantly fighting about his jealousy issues and how he is treating me, going through my phone, watching the clock if I leave. He has to go with me every time I leave the house. And if I manage to get out on my own, I get hundreds of texts asking if I am really doing what I said I was doing. If I get a text, he is right there reading it next to me. Asking me why is this person talking to me? If I miss his phone call, it is surely because I was busy having sex with someone else. I have to have a detailed account of everything I did each day and if my work schedule changed in any way he was sure it was because I was cheating. The fighting was endless and became more and more physical as time went on.

    I realized things were never going to be the same the day that he trapped me in the bedroom and threatened my job. He had trapped me in the bedroom before; he did it all the time. He would shut the door and block it with his body, keeping me there against my will. But that day he sat in front of the door and stared at me and said "if you leave me, I will hurt myself and then call the police and tell them that you did it to me." And I sincerely believed him. He knew I wouldn't risk being arrested and fired. And I knew he would follow through with his threat if I tried to break up with him. I felt trapped and alone. I just wanted out. I just wanted him to go away.

    One morning I was getting ready for work and we had started arguing. I don't even remember why anymore but he was so pissed he decided he wasn't going to let me go to work. He shut our bedroom door and stood in front of it. I had to go to work so I decided I would fight my way out. I pushed passed him and opened the door and sprinted for freedom. But I still had two flights of stairs to make it down and he caught up to me immediately. He tried pulling me back upstairs, grabbing me, punching me, hitting me, kicking me, pulling my hair, ripping my clothes off me. It took me what felt like eternity to make it downstairs. I made it to the garage and hit the garage door opener. He pushed me onto the floor and stood over me. He lifted his arm like he was going to punch me. Before he could, the garage door opened and I started screaming my lungs out. He ran back inside the house and I took off for my car.

    I was scared, shaking and crying uncontrollably. I called my ex-husband, still sobbing uncontrollably, and informed him that I had yet to change my insurance policies over to my parents. I asked him if he would please take care of my parents if I died.

There were so many times that I have been trapped in rooms and held against my will, hit, slapped, pinned down, kicked, had my head whacked into something, that there is no way to count or remember distinct instances. Anything and everything set him off, however, most of the abuse I endured was when I tried to leave. Despite all this abuse, nothing prepared me for the nights that distinctly stick out in my mind as the ones I was sure I was going to die.

We were getting ready for bed and we were arguing, probably about his stupid jealousy issues. He was standing on his side of the bed and I was kneeling on top of the bed to be able to make eye contact with him. We were just arguing, nothing physical. He bends down like he is going to pick something up, or he is looking for something. I wasn't sure what he was doing. Out of nowhere he swings and punches me right in the face, right under my left eye. The force throws me back horizontally across the bed. Immediately my vision goes black and forms a tunnel that is slowly closing. I can see his silhouette standing in front of me for a second and then everything goes completely black. I can't move and can't feel anything in my whole body except for this unbearable pain coming from the left side of my face and my eye. It feels like my face is gushing blood everywhere but I have no way of knowing if that is really happening. I can hear him walk around the bed to where my head is but I can't move, can't get up, can't run away, can't scream. He grabs a chunk of my hair hard and lifts my head up. All I can think is that he is going to punch me again and if he does I will not survive it. He twists my hair as hard as he can and I feel the pain shoot through my head and he says "are you going to get up Bitch?" I lose consciousness… I wake up in the morning with the worst headache and big black eye. He tells me I should "probably ice that thing." I tell him that I thought he had killed me. He just stares at me and says "I thought so too." No emotion, no concern, no nothing in his voice. He really didn't give a shit if I was dead or not. I take a week off of work with the "flu" to hide my black eye and every day that he comes home from work he complains to me about having to see my ugly eye.

There are good times and very bad times in an abusive relationship. The good times are what make you want to stay, what make you think that maybe things will change. There is a good person in there somewhere. He buys me flowers and chocolates. He tells me I am the most beautiful woman he has ever seen. He tells me he is sorry. That he will NEVER hurt me again. He tells me he loves me, wants to marry me, we try to plan a future together…

We had a talk a week or so before the last assault about the state of our relationship and where it was going. I told him that he had many wonderful qualities, and that was the truth. He would make a great partner, and husband but he HAD to deal with his demons. He had to deal with his anger issues, his jealousy, and his abusive ways. He agreed. He acknowledged that he had a problem and he needed to fix it. He said it was up to me to give him MORE TIME to deal with his issues…putting the blame back on me, not officially owning up to what he needed to do. I told him if he didn't start making changes by our one year anniversary that I was leaving. I had no idea how I was going to get out, but I was going to get out.

The final assault was the eye-opener that I needed to just get out. We had been arguing all day again about his jealousy issues and who was texting me and why were they texting me and was it because I was having sex with them? I tell him to leave and that I am done. And this time he actually starts to take his things and load them in his car. I feel relieved. Is it really going to be this easy? I didn't think so. He tells me he has taken my money, cash I had kept in the closet for a debt I had to pay around $1300. I was furious. I knew he would find a way to stay, to threaten me. I tell him I am calling the police, ignoring the fact that he is probably going to run off and harm himself and get me arrested for domestic violence. I am too angry to think it through. I tell him I am calling the police and reporting my money as stolen. He pushes me down and slams my head into the floor. He pins me down and starts to strangle me, hands wrapped around my neck as tight as he can. I can't breathe. I think this must be it, I am going to die right here in my kitchen. I stare into his eyes, those blue eyes that I used to think were so beautiful, and I see nothing. NOTHING. There is no soul in this man. There is nothing in there at all. He has no expression on his face. He really doesn't care. He really wants me dead. Somehow I get up and run to my phone. I don't know if he let me go or I pushed my way up but I got up, grabbed my phone and ran out of the house. I called a friend. I had never called anyone ever before during an assault. Now he has to deal with someone else knowing our business and he starts to calm down. Then he tells me, "it's ok baby, I will give you back your money if you just come inside. Just come inside and talk to me please." I go back inside and he returns my money. He keeps asking me to tell my friend that I am fine but I refuse to. I tell him I won't tell her I am fine until I know for a fact that I am fine. He tells me that none of this would have happened if I hadn't upset him and ruined his day. Could I please apologize for making him angry?? So I do just to keep the peace, to keep him from exploding again… Sorry that I made you strangle me….

That phone call to my friend saved my life. The next day she confronted me and tells me I am not going anywhere until I explain what the hell was going on. And I knew I had to. I told her everything that happened and she recommends going to our supervisor to inform him of my situation. Because he had threatened to harm himself and have me arrested for DV, I felt I had to inform my superiors of what was going on. Especially if he followed through with his threat and I ended up arrested during my escape. They also asked me to speak with DV detectives, so I went home early and met with them. They wanted to see my apartment. They took pictures of all the holes he had punched in the wall, my bruises, took my statement. Then they give me the worst news ever….this is a mandatory arrest and they will be taking him into custody. I panicked. He is going to kill me now for sure. There has to be some way that I can escape without him being arrested!? The detectives tell me there is no way around it. But they can time it right, so that he gets picked up after they know I am safely out of the house.

Four days after he strangled me in our kitchen, I escaped. I told him I was going to work like I did every single day. After I was sure he was at work, I returned with a U-haul and a wonderful group of friends who cleared out my home in about two hours. I stored everything in a storage unit and my friend let me stay with her for a month until I got myself situated. After I got everything out of the home, the detectives called me and said they were ready to arrest him. He was picked up that very same day; arrested right in front of our home. He was charged with assault in the fourth degree and strangulation. He never had a chance to go inside and see that I was already gone. He never had any idea where I went.

It has been seven months since I escaped him. There have been many rough days and every emotion in the book to make it to where I am now. He took his case to trial, but I bravely faced him. I told my story. He was convicted. I know now that the person that I was in love with wasn't a real person at all. I know what love is and what it is not. I am stronger now than I ever have been before. I can see red flags and I am not afraid to avoid people who don't feel right. I am happier now than I have been in a long, long time. No one deserves to be manipulated, controlled, or abused. I am truly free in every sense. I can do whatever I want, whenever I want. There is no more walking on eggshells for fear that I am going to do something wrong. Or that something is going to happen out of my control that I am going to get in trouble for.

It is so amazing and wonderful to adjust to newfound freedom. Seven months later and I still get excited that I can move freely from room to room in my new home whenever I want to. That I can text my friends and no one is going to accuse me of cheating. That I can go hang out with my friends and no one will be texting me demanding to know what I am doing and when I will be coming home. There is no one who is going to hit me, or call me names. I have so much to be grateful for. I am alive. If you are in an abusive relationship don't be afraid to ask for help. It will be the scariest road you will travel, but your life is worth it. There is light at the end of the tunnel. There is life after abuse.

👑 **Survivor: L. P.**

My children, My everything

Boxes and bags all packed to go,
To our clean fresh start, I told you so
A life of laughter, hopes and dreams,
instead of it falling apart at the seams
No more hurt, no more pain,
it'll never go back, never again
Wiping the memories at times is tough,
and sometimes the road still feels long and rough.

Sometimes it's hard and the days are long,
I try not to waiver, I need to be strong
To give you the chances and choices in life,
to fill it with happiness, and no more strife
three beautiful babies to love and adore,
with each passing day I love you even more
Helping you grow, learn and play,
my 3 lifesavers I just want to say...
I'm proud of you all and how far you've come,
You're my light my life, my everything...
Love mum

THE MONSTER

This is my story, so much to tell,
as I claw my way from the depths of hell.
Anger and hurt in a box under the bed,
but somehow the Monster rears its head
Out of the blue it's there in my face,
a false sense of security you take its place
It grasps me tight and doesn't let go,
doesn't let me forget those days ago
It swears, it shouts, it hurts it chokes,
lost count of the times my heart its broke
I'm running it's chasing please let me be
I can't take no more, no more not me
I stumble and trip as I pick up the pace,
the anger and evil is etched on your face
The strength of its claws it holds so tight,
I'm paralyzed with fear, it'll be a long night

Vile words and actions cut like a knife,
but surely not for the rest of my life?
Get back in the box so I can close the lid,
so scared right now I feel like a kid
I'll make you a deal, a bargain a plea,
get back in the box I need to be free
Free from the past, the torture the pain,
you're under my skin, you crawl through my veins
You twist, you turn you hiss and you spit,
my soul laid bare, my heart is split
Leave it please where it belongs, in the past
Let me move forward, and be free at last
I'm hurt, I'm torn crazy angry and mad,
I want to be me, feel good, and not bad
Keep the lid on the box, please let it stay,
I'm rebuilding my life, I'll get there one day
Need to pack it away, tie it tight,
because out of this darkness there has to be light
My heart shattered, my soul so sore,
I'm tying it tight till it hurts no more
Back under the bed where it belongs,
give it time I need to be strong
The monster will stay in the box under the bed,
and HE will no longer invade my head
My thoughts and feelings and head will be clear,
and I'll forget the price I paid so dear
With hard work, support,
with love and care....I'll peek under the bed...
and the box won't be there.

♛ **Survivor: Leah Hughes**

* * *

He swept me off my feet in June. He had this amazing tan skin and brown eyes a tattoo that covered his arm all the way to his elbow. He took my breath away in more ways than one. I should have known something wasn't right when he pushed himself into my life, but how was I to know any different. I had the rose colored glasses on, nothing Christopher did could be wrong; or so I thought.

As the months rolled by the lies started piling up. I couldn't believe anything out of his mouth, but that didn't stop me from pushing forth. We found a house together and moved in. That's when I found out that I was pregnant. He was beyond ecstatic. That's all he could talk about, was becoming a father. We found out it was a girl and named her Alyssa Korine Olson. This is when it became more than just him being vocal. He shoved me down 18 stairs. I remember closing my eyes and holding onto my stomach as I tumbled down every single step. You know the hardest thing to do is give heaven back its miracle before you could even get a chance to really love it. As I laid on the bottom step he stood over me on his phone, "Hey mom we are having a baby I'm so excited her name is Alyssa." He acted like he just didn't shove me down the steps like nothing happened. I laid there on the bottom step over night while he kicked me and pulled me by my hair. I remember crying so much the tears burned my face. I called 911 the next morning, but I forgot that he got the alerts sent to his phone as he was fire EMS. A man supposed to save lives just killed his unborn child, and beat his wife senseless. I told my first lie, I tripped down the steps. Covered in bruises and a neck brace I'm sure it wasn't hard to detect I was full of it.

Now as if this wasn't bad he started cheating on me and draining our bank accounts. He would take my car and stay gone all night. One night he called me from a bar and I went to get him. That's not how it went down, I got to the bar in time for him to push me onto the fire chief so he could move up in the fire department. I finally got him out of the bar and he tossed my keys on the ground and jumped in his car and tore off into the night. He was so intoxicated, I finally caught up to him going between 85-95 MPH that's when he lost control of the car sparks started flying and the car swerved all over the road. I remember screaming his name and slamming on my breaks. His car slammed into a guardrail and he almost flipped. I could see smoke coming from the car and I ran to grab my husband out of the car that was about to catch ablaze. This is the night he told me I deserved an upstanding gentlemen, not him. Later this night he punched me in the back 15 times knocking the wind out of me. I called my children father that next morning and told him what happened. He said it was fine not to come get the kids just to figure out what was going on with my husband. He threw a glass vase at me that afternoon for "letting him drive drunk".

At this point in my marriage he has beat me, choked me slapped me and even hit not one but both of my kids. I needed to leave I needed to find an out. I was so scared that I couldn't even open my mouth to tell people what was going on. This one night after I declared I would leave him I would work my butt off and save enough to run. In the coming months he performed CPR on me for the fun of it, I ended up throwing up blood. He choked me and there in that moment as I felt the air leaving my body I knew this was it. My oldest daughter came in the room and saw him on top of me. She began hitting him in his back and saying, "Stop leave my mama alone." There in that moment I knew my baby would watch this monster kill me. She was going to be stuck in this house with him alone. He eased up off my neck to shove my child and in that instant I scratched him got up and ran from the house with my two children.

As the days went on the cheating did to. The backlash from his new lovers attitude would come home to me and I would get punched in the back of the head, or my head slammed into the wall. His new trick was speeding and slamming on the breaks in the car or weaving in and out of traffic. The weeks carried on I slowly lost weight due not eating. I was weak and he knew it.

I was tossed out of a moving car on a back road and left for dead. I was told he would kill me. I get the question a lot, "Why did you stay" well here it is. I stayed because I was afraid he would kill me or my children as I watched him kill a dog and throw its lifeless body in the woods. The police did nothing so what would they do for me? I stayed because nobody believed me. He drained my bank account in was negative $2,589.75. I had nothing. I was later arrested for second degree assault. I protected myself and in the end the police believed him as I had blood trickling down my chest and hair ripped out. He told me later that he had me arrested and taken out of the house so he could bring his "lover" over. He said he had no "desire" for me.

In the coming weeks I needed surgery and he was there for me took great care of me. He even came home and found me unconscious in the bathroom with throw up all over the apartment. He called 911 and had me taken in. He cared for about 2 weeks then the beatings started again. He broke our bed and slammed my face into our floor heater. He put his hands around my throat and squeezed as tight as he could. At this point I was ready to die. I didn't fight it I just laid there. I started bleeding so much from my surgery that he stopped. There was blood all over me and him. The cream colored carpet had my blood all over it. He threw a scrub brush at me told me to clean it like the good bitch I was.

Now at this point I had saved enough money in a new bank account I could make it alone; I wasn't scared no more. He came home wasted after work and became instantly mad over a lawn mower. He tore off the shed door by the hinges and slung it across the yard and he grabbed the gas can and started to pour it all over my tiny apartment I texted my best friend and told her to call 911 and hurry to come to me before he kills me. This time might be it. He dumped gasoline all over me and stood there saying he was going to set me on fire. That he would kill me nobody would miss me. Thank god my friend showed up when she did because she knocked the lighter out of his hand. The police showed up as well as my landlord.

I finally got away! He then started stalking me showing up at work or parking outside of my apartment blasting his music. I went into hiding. Nobody knew where I lived or had my new number. He was out of my life. I eventually got my divorce and moved on romantically with my life.

I have never felt So loved or cherished. I found a man that loves me for all my issues and holds me close when he knows I'm having a hard time. Now if you asked me what was my mistake I would tell you it was not pacing myself not seeing through the lies. If you asked me what helped me get out I would tell you church. The power of prayer and the pastor at the church I was going to. I never reported any of the abuse because nobody believed me. My ex-husband had the gift of gab he could sell sand to the beach. I did find a domestic violence website and the group on Facebook called Domestic violence support, as well as the local health department for therapy. I also looked into the domestic violence crisis hotline; coalition against domestic violence.

I did not let domestic violence claim my life. I did have to be placed on medication because I developed PTSD from the abuse and horrid acts done. I can't sleep most nights due to the horrible night terrors. I cry in my sleep wake up screaming. I can't watch certain movies and I lost a lot of "friends". I am not the same person I was before. I always look for my closest exit I am not the go getter I once was. I analyze every male I come into contact with.

If I could give someone words of wisdom on how to handle a situation like this, I would tell them to take it serious and try and get help, don't be afraid to ask for help. I developed my own page for domestic violence and I also sell self-defense items. I will never be a victim again, and I want to help as many as I can.

♛ **Survivor: Ashely Morgan**

* * *

When I was 18, I met a man, he swept me off my feet. After a month I moved in with him. I was separated from my husband and had a six month old son. About a month after I moved in with him he slapped me across my face, I was shocked. He apologized and begged me to stay. About six months later I got pregnant with our son together. He had slapped & shoved me several times but begged me to stay & said he'd never do it again. When I was five months pregnant. I was taking a bath, he came in, and was drunk. He accused me of cheating, and tried to drown me but his dad came in so he left.

I left him the next day. I moved in with my parents. When our son was three months old, he called me drunk saying he was in the woods at my parents house and when somebody walked out of our house he was going to kill them. We then heard a gunshot. My daddy worked offshore and it was only my mom, my boys, my younger brother, and I there. Mom went out the back door, shot into the woods about 10 times yelling " Did I hit you, you sob?" We heard him yelling back. He threatened my little brother so I went back to keep my family safe.

That night he wanted just us to go riding and left my son with his parents. He was drinking and we went to the sand pits. He pulled me out of the truck, beat me for leaving & tied me to a tree in the woods, raped me & left. A young couple found me the next morning and called the cops. An ambulance came, he heard I was found & came there. He got to me and told me, if I told he did that he would kill our son. I told the cops I was drunk and went off with a guy I met in a bar and didn't know his name.

For about two months he was the perfect husband. Then one night he brought a friend of his home with him, sent my son to spend the night with his parents. He and his friend rapped me all night. I had 2 black eyes, a busted mouth, a broken nose and a fractured tailbone from that night. The next morning my son came home, and I wouldn't let him in our house & told him to go to his grandparents next door. His grandpa came and I let him in. He cried with me seeing me that way. My ex was in the tub. I told my ex-father-in-law to take my son to my parents, and tell them all I loved them and was sorry.

My parents took my oldest son away from me because of him previously, but I still stayed because I knew he would kill somebody in my family. I was going to kill myself when I heard my son leave. My Ex came out of the bathroom, pulled me off the couch by my hair, and into the yard. I pushed him down and ran toward the neighbors house, he picked up a piece of firewood threw it at me then an axe, his sister came out of her house with a shotgun and threatened to shoot him. I ran as fast as I could. I got to the neighbors house, she saw my face, let me in, locked the door and called the cops. He came to her house and busted the glass out if the window. Her boyfriend pulled up and he ran back.

I called the store where I knew my son was at and told them to hide him. My Ex went by there and the owner went outside with a gun, and made him leave. He left. The cops came. An ambulance brought me to the hospital where I stayed for 2 days. My Ex was arrested a week later with his girlfriend.

I had to testify against him. He stayed in prison for 14 years. He is out now, living 10 miles from me. Our son hates him and has three kids now. I remarried a wonderful man and he is my kids father. My husband is the best Dad, and Grandpa to all of my children, and grandchildren. I pray no woman has to go through this but I know they do.

Survivor: Gail P.

* * *

I had what is known as the trifecta of abuse. You see, I had lived in abusive situations for over 20 years. Most recently was 15 years with the same man. Although I had accepted Christ years earlier, my lifestyle was not that of a Christian. In fact, it was that of a non-believer. My life was consumed with wanting to be accepted and loved that I clung and attracted people that were toxic in nature. It was not until I was out of my toxic relationships that I realized that I was gravitating towards individuals that really and truly felt worse about themselves than I did. They needed me as much as I thought I needed them.

For me going to bars was the IN thing to do. Everyone is always laughing and having a good time in a bar, right? WRONG! People in bars are usually lonely, depressed, down on their luck and feel that they are not worth anything other than the next drink, in the hopes it will make them feel better and they could possibly be happy. I was such a person.

When I met my now ex-husband, it was in a bar. At first everything seemed too good to be true that I had found someone that wanted to be around me and seemed to really care for me. By the time I realized what type of person he really was, it was too late. I was so drawn into his schemes that I was literally blind to it. I had become so dependent upon him that I didn't think I could make it on my own and the fear of being alone, yet again, was stronger that the horrible things I was enduring. I just kept thinking that if I could only love him enough, he would change. Another false perception. Although I didn't know it at the time, but I was already being brainwashed into believing that if I left him, he would hurt me or my family. So I stayed.

Now the physical abuse began. At first it was threats to hit me, and then he did. Then there was the choking, and holding me down so that I could not move, while screaming at me about how useless I was. One of his favorite things to say to me was "You wouldn't make a pimple on my Mom's ass." Let me tell you that hearing that just cuts right through you.

His drinking got heavier and heavier, as did mine to simply deal with the pain and emotional trauma I was experiencing. I am not proud of the fact that I was basically on the cuff of becoming an alcoholic. He began drinking for 18 hours, 24 hours and up to 36 hours straight. I would try my hardest to not do anything, say anything or even look at him wrong to avoid setting him off. I never knew when it was going to happen. Exhaustion began to take its toll on me and if I fell asleep when he didn't think I should, bam.

One night, September 17, 2008, he had been drinking for 36 hours. It was his birthday. I decided to go to bed and I really don't know exactly how long I was asleep that he came into the bedroom, got the .38 pistol and fired two shots at me, at my head, while I was sleeping. Those bullets missed my head by 6 and 8 inches. I have never been so scared in my entire life. At the time we had a waterbed and of course the bullets punctured the bed and water began pouring out of a king size bed. Of course to him it was my fault that he shot at me, I went to bed and left him all alone in the living room. I had to clean up the mess. Luckily we had a carpet cleaning machine so I was able to suck up the water over several trips to empty the bucket in the tub. During this time he just sat in the living room staring off into nowhere. We had a fire pit out back on our deck so I asked him if I could go outside and have a fire. Luckily he agreed. I started the fire and came in for some water and realized that he had gone to sleep in the other room. What a relief. I went back outside to sit by the fire and began to cry. I have never cried so hard as I did that night.

That night the sky was completely clear, no clouds anywhere. The moon was just about full and the stars were absolutely gorgeous. I finally stopped crying and was sitting by the fire and began to call out to God to please save me. Asking God to rescue me from my situation seemed the only thing I could do and the only thing that gave me any sort of comfort. It was then that I looked up into that beautiful night sky and there saw a cloud with the face of a man in it. I could not believe what I was seeing. This man's face was older, seasoned so to speak, and seemed very kind and peaceful. It is hard to explain. I bowed my head and began to cry again and ask God that if that cloud was a sign from Him to somehow, let me know. I didn't know what else to ask. I dried my tears with my shirt and looked up again at the cloud to see the face. This time the face in that wonderful cloud was smiling, actually smiling. Well, the waterworks started all over again. It was then that I hit my knees, and then was flat on my stomach on the deck, bawling my eyes out and thanking God for letting me know that He was there. Once I was able to get myself together, and stop crying, I realized in my heart that everything was going to be ok. That I was going to be ok. I don't know how I knew it at the time, but I knew it. I call that night my God Cloud Night.

 After that horrible night, it was about 7 months later. It was Sunday, April 19, 2009. I asked him if I could go to church. He said yes. Again he had been up all night long drinking. I went to church and it was wonderful. It was as if the sermon was for me. After the service I decided to go to Sunday School and that was great too. I went home and he was furious that I was gone so long and wanted to know where I was, even accused me of running around on him. So once again the screaming and yelling began and that's when I saw that he had taken everything out of the refrigerator and thrown it out on the back deck and said I made him do it because he didn't know where I was. I told him I was going to go for a drive and he said no. He unplugged the garage door opener so I couldn't open the door, I climbed up while he was in the bathroom and was starting to drive away when he came out and started shooting at me and screaming to get back inside. I drove away, tires squealing all the way out of the drive. I was so scared.

 I called my parents after a little while and decided that I was not going back, and they drove to Knoxville to get me. I went and got as much money as the ATM would let me, filled up my tank in the car, picked up food and found a motel that was about 10 miles away and paid cash for the room. When I got into the room, I just let everything out and cried for about 3 hours. I then took a hot bath and seemed to help calm me down. My parents arrived about an hour after that and I fell apart once again. During all this time he was calling me on my cell phone and leaving very, very horrible messages of what he was going to do to me and to my family. He even threatened to kill my dog.

We went to the social services the next day and they helped me file an Order of Protection against him with the help of the police. We left Knoxville for South Carolina. I only had to go back to go to court and to get what little he allowed me take from the house. He of course could not be there and had to leave while I was there. That I was grateful for. I have never been back since.

I have been living violence free for almost 4.5 years now. I have started my own ministries called Faith Driven Ministries SC (www.faithdrivenministriessc.com) and I have become a speaker for Sistercare, an organization dedicated to helping victims of domestic abuse/violence. It is my desire to use my ministry to also help victims of domestic abuse/violence.

               Survivor: Lily Rose

* * *

In 1999, I was with a man; we loved each other, young love, and my first love so we bonded really well. I was at university and he really encouraged studying, which I found totally inspiring towards my work. I also supported his business venture.

He had his troubles he found tough as a teenager to deal with break-up of his parents' marriage, he went off the rails. He experimented with far too many class A drugs. We decided to go on a two week holiday to the South of France, I felt before we left he was acting very strange waking up in the middle of the night, and laughing hysterically which freaked me out.

During a very long drive to the campsite the van got stuck in sand, fortunately a local stopped to help, and we nearly had an accident. He decided to stop in a car-park for a break for the remainder of night. He got out and left me in the dark and I was wondering what have I done? It was a horrible situation but I tried to rest. In the morning we continued the journey eventually arriving at the camp-site. It should have been an exciting time but he got out of the vehicle and began cursing, much to my embarrassment. 'Don't you fucking talk to me, stay away from me you fucking cunt'. Stuck, what could I do? In a different country feeling very scared.

One night he lost the plot once more, so when I approached him, not argumentatively, and said 'Daniel, what have I done and why are you acting like this?' I was getting ready for bed standing half dressed in my bra. He stood up and pushed me so hard that I fell into the kitchen area in the tent and smashed against the pots and pans which made a real racket. I picked myself up crying hysterically. The people next door came to see what had happened. The next thing security came with dogs and he was ordered off the campsite. I had to pretend that I had left and hid all of my belongings in the tent next door. Advised by the owners as I could not go anywhere with him. I was petrified.

In the morning I set off to the beach for the day. I had to make that horrible call to my mum and dad to bail me out and book me a flight home. I was distraught. The love of my life treating me this way. A 2 1/2 year relationship ending like this, and I had to go home alone. I found out in the following weeks his mum had to get him sectioned in a mental hospital and was diagnosed with paranoid schizophrenia.

Three weeks later it was my birthday and went into town to a club with a friend to celebrate. I was pretty miserable and not looking for anyone. Isn't that what they say? You meet someone special when you're not looking? I bumped into a guy I knew from when I was at school out with his mates, one of which, a schoolmate of mine was going out with 5 years previous. I felt safe but it was not love at first sight. I was vulnerable.

He was celebrating his birthday too! I thought he was lying but turned out we were born on the same day he a year older than me!! It's not every day you meet someone born the same day as you. We found out that my mum and aunt knew his Nan and aunt and both of our mums were born into large families, one of seven. Even both of our grandparents have plots opposite each other in the cemetery. There were some coincidences that felt special and safe after the ordeal I had been through with my ex. We began to see each other and I pretty much moved in with him when he rented a room in a house shared with his mates. He was a taxi driver and he would pick me up and flash the cash, wine and dine, and spoil me. We stayed in nice hotels some nights, and he made me feel special, Something my previous boyfriend never did.

The very early signs were not something I could just run away from. They just seemed like a natural response. I remember he particularly hated it when I chose to stay up partying with his mates and girlfriends after he had decided to go to bed, not for long as I knew my place. I was sometimes a bit late getting to his place, and he would absolutely despise it, having a go at me for being half an hour late! He could not let his true colors show because the house was full. He and some others failed to pay the rent and it was time for him to leave. In fact they all did. I later found out that it all went to court and one of the nicer guys, Gary paid the outstanding balance never to have the money returned!

It was time for me to return to my final year at university 200 miles away. It was hard to leave after finding a new love! Long distance relationships can be kind of hard, and always leave you wondering whether that person will stay faithful. He actually drove 200 miles to see me a number of occasions, but he struggled and made it difficult when he wasn't with me, calling in the early hours sobbing on the phone saying 'I can't do this I want you here with me'. It was hard for me trying to finish my final year dealing with the emotional turmoil.

Time for graduation, and things seemed to move to the next level in terms of the abuse and natural progression of the relationship. By this time he had moved into a flat and I basically moved in. We dabbled in drugs, but I really wanted to continue my design career, proving difficult when all the focus seemed to be aimed at him, whilst I found myself always encouraging and supporting his new business venture. His attitude changed when he had a drink, and he became more controlling and verbally abusive always accusing me of sleeping around whilst at university.

I found myself constantly having to prove my innocence, and defend myself. He broke my mobile phone to pieces by throwing it in the street when he was in a drunken rage, accusing me of something. It was like he used the thought of me being unfaithful as an excuse to abuse. When we went out he hated me talking to his friends, or anyone really. He used to watch me like a hawk, and if I did or said something out of line it would be used as another excuse to abuse. He stole the fun from my life, but was very gradual; once drink flowed the accusations seemed to creep in. I stopped going out with him because every time I did he would accuse me of something! Getting hold of me by the scruff and scrunching his face up I would look around to see who was watching feeling embarrassed, I used to walk out and walk back to the flat alone many occasions.

It is so true, they say people who are being abused do not realize it as abuse. Caught up in the haze of the moment fogs your mind feeling overwhelmed by the accusations. Not until the 36th time, the victim contemplates ringing the police for help. That was me as crazy as it all sounds, call me stupid? I just did not think it was abuse way back then. It took me a very long time to acknowledge this as abuse. He seemed to do it only once he had a drink and that became the blame. Even when he tried to strangle me fully clothed in the bath after a night out because he accusing of something untoward. I'm glad to say to say that I broke his thumb and needed an operation on the ligament. Bruises around my neck and I was feeling bad because he needed an operation. I always tried to address the abuse to him and I said I really don't want to live this way, he would agree and say I love you sorry then we would have sensual sex and sweep it under the carpet.

One night he got my clothes and threw them out of the window and basically threw me down the stairs and out into the street 12 o'clock at night. Where could I go? I could not admit this to my parents, the shame of it. I think I went to a friend's place up the road where I was safe, as her partner had rescued her from a violent relationship, and would not condone such behavior. I think the next day I got my stuff and went to my parents. They thought we just had a volatile relationship I found it so hard to admit such behavior to them. He begged, apologized he loved me and all the other things. Would you believe from this period we actually went on to buy a house together. I say we but he was blacklisted and only with my credit scoring I was able to get a mortgage. By this time I had a steady job at a local hospital, and managed to get a place with the key workers scheme. My mum really encouraged us with the move I guess she was proud but I got into a lot of debt. Needing a massive loan to even move in. I got credit cards, bought flooring for the living room, a couch on finance. He made me believe that he would help me financially, but when it came down to it was an empty promise. I was living on empty promises. He needed a brand new car, he and his dad were not able to get credit so guess who did! Again he told me that he would pay the finance but it was hit and miss.

Excited to move into our new home beginning a new phase of our lives hoping all that stuff would be left behind. He used to say to me oh, take me away from these people who are dragging me down they are not real friends, they like it when things go wrong. They only like me when I'm down on my luck which kind of made me feel settled about the move. We decorated and cooked together things were good when we worked together we had the same tastes. Things were okay but began to realize that he was out more frequently drinking with his friends. I would cook food for both of us and would call him, and he would say he would be home soon but began to stay out longer and at closing in he rolled.

A prisoner in my own home, he would go out straight from work and I would sit alone at home, and cry and get so down. Struggling to survive financially, and was just existing, certainly not living. Past experiences put me off going out with him as always turned into a night of drama. This control took over my life I had no money to do anything because everything earned went to bills and debt. How could I go out consumed with debt and he continued to swan around earning just what he could to squander on drink.

I was stuck. I had to even scrap my car, could not get it fixed, or afford to even run it. I traveled to work by bus. He could not even pick me up from work instead he would go to the pub. It got to the point where we could not pay for his car any longer and had to give it up to auction. My mum kindly gave me her old car because she thought it would help which gave me more freedom.

Five years down the line and in that time I can honestly say that I did not go out with friends I did not have many by then. The debt became too much and I needed help; my mum was my only savior, the only one I could ask my life line. She cleared a credit card for me, I still had three more to go. I was in about £25,000 of debt it was an extremely distressing time. He even persuaded me to remortgage the house to clear some accounts, which only seemed to build up again.

A girl from work asked if I would like to go into town for a drink, I accepted and he went to a friend's party. I foolishly said, why don't you join me when you finish, call me you know where I will be. I bumped into a guy, friends used to knock about together and guess what? He pounced on me when I was talking to him, and started accusing this poor guy. He took me outside the bar and took me by the scruff of the neck and started to snarl in my face. I think the bouncers got involved and told him to go. My friend convinced me to come back in and have a drink. I did not want to go home. I felt something was not right and was scared. I got a lift home and he was nowhere to be seen.

I went to get onto Facebook, but the door flew open, my heart dropped and he ran up the stairs, started smashing my keyboard up, Threw me onto the bed and put his knees on my arms above my head really hard pushing down hard crying hysterically I had actually done nothing. Pushing me down the stairs, all I needed was my keys and get the hell out of there but he took them. He opened the front door and, pushed me into the road so hard I fell backwards, and with an almighty thud my head hit the floor. I pulled myself up and I walked, away from him.

The only place I could go was my parents a five mile walk, 2 am in the morning, and I was going. Long dark lonely roads but I was determined. I tried to call a friend but she never answered thank god I had my phone. The police called my parents and told them that my car had been found smashed up and he was charged with drink driving. My car was a Write-off. I arrived my mum was distraught but glad I was safe. In the morning my dad called the police and I made a statement. He also made me go to the doctors to check my bruises on my head and body.

That was it. No more I could take. I collected most of my stuff from the house and put it on the market to be sold. Victim support called me to offer any support, I told them we had split up, thinking I could do it on my own.

I was strong for five months. I met someone else who also had a terrible time with his ex we understood each other. But one day he said sorry babe I have to go away. And that was that. What a blow, but it was too soon. Emotions all over the place, the dominator, in time, began to sweet talk me. Manipulation crept in and we talked about the future planning things we could do together to the house. After a six month split, we moved back to the house, my dad hardly talked to me, he knew I was making a big mistake and told me so. I guess had to finalize it. My mum was there for me, I needed that. The problem with these relationships is that at times like this people cannot understand why the hell we put up with such behavior.

We decorated the bedroom really nice, and I was very pleased with the result. We were getting along better. He had a lot to deal with, as his sister had a stillbirth, and it was so sad to have to go to the funeral. His granddad died, who I quite liked as a person.

Four months later, I fell pregnant and had a beautiful little girl. He cried when she was born. He was a bit of a softy in some ways. I felt truly awful, and did not want any visitors; I had very high blood pressure and his mum even said to me in the hospital look at your hair! That was the least of my concerns.

On the journey home from hospital I realized I had made a big mistake. He did not even try the baby car seat before hand and realized the seat belt was too short. Oh fuck, this is going to be good. He hated me breast feeding because he could not control feeds, and it meant I had more contact with my baby. Every time his sister came around she said oh you're feeding again. Yep, my baby! Isn't that the most natural thing in the world, to breast feed?

I started to go out more and more with mummy friends, which he absolutely hated. He did all the food shopping and began to give me money monthly, which he had to because my maternity decreased, and bills needed to be paid. He took us away for a week's holiday. Baby only 1 year and a half, the first holiday we had in nine years. When we got there he said, I'm just going to get bottle of wine. He did not come back for three hours. I went out two nights that holiday. One night my friend came to visit as she lived nearby and he treated her to a meal, which was very nice, but when we got back and she left he began to be abusive about my parents pretending to walk like my dad calling him a fat lazy Welsh bastard. I tried to defend, but I was holding my little girl. He did it in such a way, that it was like a comedy act for the benefit of her, as a way to hide the abusive words. He came up to me and squeezed an unlit cigarette squashing it on the side of my nose. The side my daughter could not see. From that moment I hated him. I should have left him there and gone home! I began to notice the verbal abuse more now that my little girl was experiencing it too.

One day, he had been drinking, he was getting abusive holding our daughter and he pushed me onto the mattress in our bedroom, which must have been forceful as I went down and fell with the mattress, onto the floor. I was tiring of the situation it was slowly dragging me down, and I began to see it for what it was. The abuse was becoming clear to me. Shame it took so many years?

We had new neighbors move in and really got on with them, it was a 'God send'. We arranged to pop out one night. I told him of my plans as I rarely got out, he did the usual, strolled in with his dad half an hour before the planned time. I was washing up not even ready. He began to curse me which was embarrassing as the windows and back door were open. His dad was smirking cruelly as ever. 'Slag, fucking slut, what sort of mother are you, fucking druggie. What?' He threatened to call social services then actually called the police. It rang; he showed me but then hung up. His father loved to witness the abuse, he did not say one word to his son, talking to the mother of his sons child, unforgiving, to say nothing. He came up to me and said 'calm down don't get angry'. What the fuck, was he serious? CHEEK! Go on, take yourself and your son get out of my house, how dare you speak to me like that. I got my keys and went out as planned. The town was like a ghost town and I did not feel right. We got a drink and I became wheezy and I had forgot my asthma inhaler. Had to come back to get it. A police car was parked on the road, OH, has this all backfired on him! They tracked the call even though he hung up and came to check things were okay. I said I would like to talk to them and asked if they would take him away from me for the night, not feeling safe if left alone with him. Police drove him to his parents for the night, living like this is ludicrous.

I began to see it as abusive behavior/ domestic violence. Always stressed out, I could not sit down and relax anymore. I was wired all the time; I became resentful of doing house chores day in day out the stress of my baby. I was contacted by my health visitor who wanted to come to the house and check things were okay. I did it without him knowing and opened up to her told her everything. She continued these visits for the next year every month. She told me to be careful and try to write things down as they happen, but hide it don't let him find it. Also, I contacted a domestic abuse helpline, and talked to the outreach team. They seemed to know the situation, it felt like they were on my side, it made sense, they took notes documented things that happened. I began to feel stronger as I was telling things. They said, no, this behavior is not acceptable.

At this point, my last relationship came to mind and kept thinking I hope he is okay? I had unanswered questions from my past. Was it me that made him like this? Why does my present partner treat me this way? He used to care, right? A friend knew him too, and contacted him on Facebook. He took my number met for coffee and talked. He was like I remember a nice guy. He had a break down way back then and I guess he flipped, just a shame that I was in the firing line!

My current partner searching my phone convinced he would find something, he found a text from Daniel. Oh, he went mad. I was so worried, I called my mum to come over because I was not sure how it would pan out. He had been to the pub and was drunk he was angry; I was shaking in my boots. Horrible night, I tried to explain that I needed to close my past, and put it to sleep. He got angrier, telling my two year old daughter 'mummy likes sucking black cocks'. It was appalling and I had enough but the abuse just got worse and worse from then on, I broke the control rules I had friends, I had contacted my ex, I was going out.

I took my notes from that time and would like to write a snippet from that and share the things that happened on a daily basis:

"Come home after being in the pub, almost nightly, when I was trying to put my daughter to bed, saying my friend, whose daughter was born the same day as mine, we became friends, was a 'slag, boring'. I went into the bathroom to get this hostility out of Brooke's room. He said I swear to god I would smash you about. I said go on do it! Get out of my face.

He interrogates after verbal abuse he went downstairs and making my daughter laugh but really he was suggesting he would 'slit my throat' obviously she was too young to understand.

I was giving my daughter some milk and she was saying Daddy and getting distressed so I said she wants to kiss you goodnight and he came up and kissed her.

It took me about an hour to put her to bed after all that. He also reckoned that he was recording everything too and he had her passport in his pocket and was saying they are going away.

Luckily my neighbor was out in their garden so they lightened the mood. He was sorting out his medication box, banging things about and I went down and asked him to keep the noise down. It is not fair to B to try to go to sleep whilst that entire racket is going on. He said I'm going, Blah! Blah! Wish he would go and leave me and B in peace but B hears him say it then clings onto him and cries.

When she finally went to sleep I went downstairs and he was not there. I had a chat with my neighbor in the garden then he came in again. He was being mean to me about my trousers. We were supposed to be having a glass of wine, me and George (neighbor). She gave me a beer and a plant for looking after her cat last weekend. I went in to do the washing up and he was saying I was going to get a shock on Monday and he is going to wipe the house clean. I had enough and went to bed at 9:30 PM.

He came to bed about 10 and wallowing in hate got his phone and told me he was texting someone to break Daniels legs and chop his fingers. I just lay there listening to my heart beat faster. Then he got up and took the duvet from me and said I'm going to sleep downstairs. So I got my dressing gown and put it over me.

My cat came in the cat flap and he threw something at him and shooed him away. Willbo Was scared and ran back out. I just thought you horrible man. After about ten minutes he came upstairs dumped duvet on the bed put the light on and crouched down to the bed where I lay dug his head into my arm as I put my head underneath the dressing gown. I held my arm up firm as he dug into me; he threw himself on the floor accusing me of breaking his nose. I looked at him and he was punching himself in the face. He said you have broken my nose. With that he will call the police and say I broke it.

I had enough at this point and got up and put my clothes on and said I'm going to my mum and dad's this is ridiculous by this time it was almost 11pm and have had 4hours of this treatment.

10/6/2011

Tonight I just want to go to bed before gets in. On Monday when I picked up

B the crèche were concerned about her it took three of them to calm her down. She was head butting the wall; I'm very concerned it is like the damage is done.

He came up upstairs turned the light on and said "Wakey, wakey, I know what you have been doing". Talking to all these people, I've seen all these numbers you have written down. I thought oh, great he has found something else. What could I do I denied it, "what are you talking about"? He looked in my bag to see what he could find. My heart racing and beginning to panic just wanting to relax and go to sleep. He was standing by the bed blocking the door. I got up and said this is ridiculous and probably said I'm going to call the police if you carry on. I reached for my phone, which I turned off previously because I had a feeling something may happen.

He accused me of texting whilst in bed. B woke up crying, I was shaking and crying with stress. I whispered to B " I'm sorry about this darling and tried to comfort her"

I heard him smash my phone on the floor because he could not get into it. I came downstairs and went to the landline to call the police, the line was dead. I went outside in my dressing gown and knocked on my neighbor' door, no reply. He came outside with my sim card in his hand and said "If you get her I will throw this over the fence" I said "that's blackmail". He was angry I got that glare and reluctantly went back into the house. B was crying so I went to see her. I just patted her on the back and said so sorry this is not fair.

I heard him go outside for a cigarette and was worried about him finding this book and things so I crept in the bedroom and got them. Just as I hid them under B's cot he came upstairs with my sim. He went into the bedroom and was getting some bits. He says he will leave if I call the police. How I could actually do that I don't know? He was getting angry again, I could hear him fumbling about. I was reading books to B try and get our mind off the commotion. I sat on the floor and B on the stool. He stood in the doorway, saying stuff about my sim. threats he chucked it on the floor near my hand. I reached for it and he put his foot on it. Picked it up and put it in his mouth. I will swallow it if you call the police. What? Well I can't! Getting angry and annoyed with him, beginning to grate on me.

He went into the bedroom and started to punch the wardrobe, I shouted my neighbor's name three times really loud. He was horrified. I said get out. "Oh that's great the neighbors' heard that and now they think I'm killing you." I said you may have taken my phone and landline but I have a voice and I can use it. I will go into the street if I have to. I went back to B to see if she was okay, I must have settled her about 2.30am. He packed a big bag of clothes and put them downstairs by the door. He was laying on the bed, I just went to sleep."

The next morning I met a friend and her little boy and we went swimming carrying on as normal. I needed to tell someone, my dad. When I called my mum was home. I told her. She could not believe it and she went on to tell my dad. She thought it was about time someone said something. So he called him, and said 'what's this about you destroying my sim card?'

Later that day he collected his stuff.

A week later, I was due to begin the freedom program, a help group for DV victims. It is a twelve session course, aimed at understanding the traits of the abuser, the dominator. Once the traits were understood the behavior was easier to recognize and how the patterns they come and go. Childhood experiences are very important and play a massive part of how the dominator works. My ex's sister told me how she witnessed her father smash a bottle of champagne over her mums head!!! His father taught him exactly all there is to know about abusing a woman. We have to teach our children this behavior is not tolerated, break the cycle.

Other ladies at the freedom program had, or were still going through, the same things as me. It was so helpful. Every women walking this planet needs to read the Freedom Program, it has taught me to be strong.

Three years later I have experienced every emotion possible. Desperation, I cannot do this, helplessness, scared, upset, angry, happy, love sick, needy, hurt, bitterness, resentful, tearful, shame, guilt, but one thing is for sure, I will never jump into any relationship just because I can!!!! I'm finding myself again.

Survivor: Natalia Hardly

* * *

I met my abusive partner through a friend. He had a child that was a one year old, and his ex was pregnant with another of his, when the children were one and two, their mum left them with us. We had them full time whilst living together. The abuse started after a couple of years together, and got worse when he drank. It started with bruises all over my body by being pushed, shoved, grabbed and by being thrown against things, like the cupboard. One time he threw me against the corner of a wall and that split the back of my head open and blood started pouring down.

As time went on he was sure to rip me away from everything and everyone I knew. He threw away clothes of mine he didn't like. He often called me names and was verbally abusive to me, as well as emotionally, and physically. He slowly took away all my confidence, self belief, I had very low self esteem and felt very alone. He always blamed his violence on me, saying I deserved it.. Saying that I'm not worth anything better, and after he cooled down each time he would then apologize and tell me he wouldn't do it again, the times I told him I'm leaving him and packed my bags, he would cry and beg me for forgiveness, and tell me he would change, but he never did.

Without knowing he used to follow me wherever I went. To my mum's house, to the gym, to meet friends, and on the occasion he let me go out for a drink, He would follow me then too. On the odd occasion when I did go out for drinks with friends he would follow me. He then used to start fights with men in bars/clubs that were even standing anywhere near me that he thought I was 'cheating' on him with, which I wasn't. I later found out that he had cheated on me plenty of times throughout our relationship. The two children of his that lived with us looked up to me as their 'mummy' so that was another reason I also found hard to leave.

On a number of occasions when I had been abused, I called the police, and he got arrested for his violence towards me, but every time he got let out, he'd find me. He would also threaten to hurt me, or my family, so I had to take the charges back, he also threatened me if I broke up with him, and forced me to stay with him during all this time. I was constantly scared, looking over my shoulder and never felt safe. I was scared for my family and for myself, for ages I just saw no way out.

The abusive relationship continued for a few years. The worst abuse I suffered was on Christmas Day. One year he, his two children, and I were at his parents' house, with them and their other 4 children. By the afternoon he started an argument with me, he then followed his abusive mouth with two full blown punches, one to each eye socket, I fell to the ground, he started to laugh and shouted, 'You got knocked the fuck out', as if he was proud of what he'd done, and wanted to show off in front of everyone. I called some family friends to help rescue me, it took me about 20 minutes to get out the house as he wouldn't let me out the front door, it took me promising not to call the police for him to let me out.

The next day both my eyes were completely black and blue, they had swollen so bad that I could only partly see out of one eye, after a week or so when my eyes eventually opened, you couldn't even see the white part of both my eyes, the white parts were completely blood red. Shortly after that incident he was up to his usual tricks and started following me around, throwing stones at my bedroom window in the middle of the night so he could talk to me. It got to the point where he was threatening to burn down my mum's and my dad's houses.. Their cars.. So I got back with him so I could protect my family.

Then one day, something just clicked and I knew I'd had enough and couldn't take anymore, I knew I didn't love him and felt sick every time I looked at him, he repulsed me and I couldn't stand being anywhere near him. I found the courage with the help of my family to leave him. The only safest way I could do this, was to move away without telling him, I had everything planned a month in advance, I had sorted out renting a new home half way up the country, I had a date to move in.. I broke up with him a few days before, I was leaving the area, I went to stay at my mum's during that time as she was moving with me, he was hassling me for those few days, but I didn't answer the calls, or text him back. I started to feel strong, and I saw that there could be a light at the end of the tunnel.

I was my last night at my house before moving away, I then got a call in the middle of the night, I didn't hear it go off, but when I woke up I had a voicemail. It was a police lady that had rang me, she said that he had been arrested after starting a fight with someone and that he should be let out around midday and that he just wanted me to know. I then told my mum and we knew we literally had a couple hours to finish our last bits of packing and to leave before he was let out of the cells. We made it, we moved away without him knowing anything. I felt utter relief and freedom straight away.

Now it's five and a half years on from leaving him, and moving away and I've never been happier. I have built a new life and I am surrounded by amazing people. I feel very blessed, I love my life and I am so thankful to my family for their continued support through everything. Although he still sometimes makes up many different Facebook profiles to stalk me, I just press one button to block him. I do have nightmares about it sometimes but then I wake up and realize, I am safe. I am so happy in life, and feel proud that I overcame this ordeal that I was put through.

♛ **Survivor: Stephie T** .

* * *

I was 16, living in a unit, with my brother. I had dropped out of school, and was working at an aged care home. One day, I came home to find a bunch of people and friends, who also lived in the units sitting out back drinking and having a good old time. I jumped up on the back of a Ute, (truck like car) and joined in. When a taxi pulled up, and this handsome cotton farmer jumped out, my heart started pounding and got I butterflies. I tried not to let it show. After a while I asked whose Ute I was sitting on, and he piped up and said 'That would be me'. I hinted for him to come sit with me, and he came and stood between my legs with his back to me. From that day on we were inseparable.

He was coming in town every day after work to see me, and he would stay the night, and get up at 4 a.m., to be back for work the next day. When I had time off work, I would go and stay at the farm with him. We did this for two months. Then he asked me to move in, and that he earned enough for the both of us. With that, I dropped my job, and moved in with him.

I was so in love with him. He was so nice, and charming. I felt so safe in his arms. Over the next few months I started to smoke pot with him, just for fun, till one day I was out on the tractor with him. We had a fight, and he smacked my head into the tractor door. I screamed at him, begging him, to stop the tractor and let me out. He refused until I told him I would jump out. He said, 'Wait until I get back up to the Ute, then you can'. I sat in silence, crying in shock of what just happened. We got to the Ute, he let me out, and I sped off home. I sat on the couch. I could not open my left eye so I smashed down a few hits, until I was numb all over.

I went to the bathroom to look at the damage he did. My eye was so puffed up and black, I broke down in tears again. Once I gathered up the courage,, I drove back out to him, and waited until he finished the run in the tractor. He pulled up and I hopped in and said, 'You need to take me to hospital it feels like its going to explode.' He begged for my forgiveness, and said 'I'm so sorry baby girl. I didn't mean it. I'll never do it again'. He took me to hospital, but first he stopped to talk to a mate. When his mate asked about my eye, he said I bumped it on the handle of the tractor door while getting something out the tucker box. His friend replied 'It looks like someone hit you with a baseball bat.' I just looked at my hands in my lap, and let silent tears fall.

I Told him I needed to see my mum, and he asked why. I told him the hospital will ring her since she was my next of kin. He said 'OK but don't tell her I did this. Remember the story.' I walked in to see my mum. She was behind the counter, and when she looked up at me, I could not hold my tears in any longer. She ran to me and held me tight. Her work friends told her to take a break with me. She looked at me. She said 'He did this, didn't he" I could see the rage in her eyes. I couldn't lie to her, and said 'Yes he did mum.' She said was going to kill him. I begged her not to say anything, and that he had promised to never do it again, I loved him, and that would just make it worse. She told me she won't this time, but if he did it again, she would go off on him.

We then left to go to hospital, and there was one of his friends mum working there. She came over and asked us what happened. I looked at him, and he told her the tucker box story. She said she had to take a photo, and that they have never seen a black eye so big before.

The hospital didn't do anything just said to keep an eye on it. We went home things were good for a few weeks, then it started again. It was a lot of put downs, and punches in the arms and legs, every time I said, or did, something wrong. One day, we had friends over, and he was testing out his new compound bow. He asked me to get his arrows. As I was walking to get them, he started shooting arrows at me while they all sat there laughing. I threw the arrows down, and went inside.

That night after a few bowls, and the boys were hanging out on the couch, he asked me to come into the bedroom. He said he had something to show me. Something he got when he was away a few days before hand. He gave me a nurses outfit. He told me to put it on. I refused because we had people over, but he started to get mad, so I put it on. He then threw me on the bed and raped me. I cried out, but he told me to shut up. I just cried.

When he was done, he said to get dressed, and to have a shower. When I got my cloths and went to bathroom, the boys were outside. No wonder they didn't hear my cries. After a shower, I had a few more bowls, and tried to sit but my bum was too sore. I joined everyone outside. He just looked at me, smiled, handed me a drink, and a smoke to reward me for taking it.

A few weeks later, we had a fight, and when he went to bed, I poured myself a stiff drink. He came out and said 'What, too good to drink with me?' I said 'Yep' and took a sip of my drink. He tapped the bottom of the glass so it spilled down my front. I threw the rest of the drink on him. He grabbed the cup and put it on the table, grabbed my hair, and pushed me to the ground rubbing my face in it telling me how ungrateful, and useless I am. He let me go after what felt like hours.

I tried to run to the bathroom. It was the only door in the house that locked, but he was right behind me, and pushed the door open, grabbed my throat, and pushed me to the wall. He pushed with enough force, that I smacked my head on the wall. He continued to yell abuse at me for a while. Then he had a few cones and went to bed leaving me to clean up the mess. I then had a few bowls to numb the pain, and went to bed.

One night, we had so much to drink and it was early hours of Easter morning. He was passed out on the couch. When I went to wake him, he yelled at me saying 'Fuck off you slut. Leave me alone' I got so upset. I had enough. Enough of him. enough of getting abused. enough of the pain. I grabbed a butchers knife, and ran to the bathroom. I sat behind the door with my feet on the bottom of the shower using my body to keep the door shut and started to saw at my left wrist. I lost my best friend in November the year before, and was hurting. I never had the chance to tell him I loved him, and with my boyfriend beating me up, I had enough. I just wanted to end it. I just sat there running this knife back and forth across my wrist till it was numb. I started to cut deeper and deeper, balling my eyes out, thinking of finally finding peace.

  He came to the door and tried to open it. He pushed on the door until it opened. He looked at my arms and started going out of his head, confused as to why I would do something like this. I told him I wanted peace. He grabbed me and held me in his arms. I told him what he said to me when I tried to wake him up, he said he was sorry, and turned the shower on. He hopped in fully clothed with me, and washed my arm. He told me it needed stitches, and he called an ambulance. He couldn't drive because was still drunk. I begged him not to let them take me away. He said 'baby girl no one will take u from me, I promise.' He wrapped a towel around my wrist and carried me to the couch where he sat with me on his lap, and cradled me till the ambulance came.

  There were three cop cars and two ambulances. They took me away after talking to me about what happened. I went to hospital and they called my mum and she met me there and sat with me crying as they stitched me up. She said 'You know they have to take you away.' I knew. I went quietly, and I was away for about a month. Once they released me, he came and picked me up. We went to his mums house for a few weeks before we went home.

  Once home he started again. Back to making me have sex with him four times a day, and beating me again. One day he got up one day to go to work. Once he left, I pumped a few hits off the bowl into me, and went back to bed. A few hours later he came home and told me to get up and dressed. We were going out. I told him I needed a shower, a coffee, and smoke first. We argued for a bit, and when I seen him get up, I curled in a ball on the bed. He punched me 3 times in the back of the head as hard as he could. All the while yelling abuse at me. He then sat on the couch in our room and started smoking. I got up crying, and told him he was an asshole. I started to go up stairs, but he followed me, still yelling at me. I stopped halfway up the steps, and turned around, just as he pulled my legs out from under me.

I kicked him in the nuts and ran to the bathroom. I tried to keep the door shut. It didn't lock so he barged right in. I put my hands up so he didn't hit my face, but he grabbed my hand's and started punching me in the face with my own hands. Still yelling abuse at me. He eventually let me go after he split my lip, and threw me at the sink. He told me to clean myself up and walked away. I grabbed my smokes and phone and went to sit outside to have a smoke. He followed, and took my smokes and phone, and said you don't deserve them. I went and sat in the lounge room. He still followed me. He started smacking me round the head and all up in my face yelling at me.

I was so scared that I was dry heaving and kept telling him over and over if he didn't leave me alone i was going to vomit all over the floor. He kept going for a bit then went to toilet. While he was there, I grabbed the smokes and my phone from the bench. He was on his way out of the bathroom when he seen me just exit the door. He started running after me. I tried to make it up the hill to my dog but he caught up to quick so I just dropped to the ground and curled up in a ball. He grabbed my legs and started dragging me around the back yard by them while yelling abuse at me.

Eventually he let me go and told me to get in the Ute. I walked over to the Ute. I still had my phone on me so when he realized he left his keys inside, I called the police begging them to save me. He came out and realized who I was talking to. He started yelling at me saying 'You fuckin cunt. How dare you.' and then 'Baby girl, I love you' and he just kept repeating those two things, over and over until I was off the phone. He calmed down and begged me not to send him to jail. He kept saying 'You know what they will do to me in there, don't you?' I didn't answer him.

Once the cops got there, I told them it was only a verbal fight. The cop said that he could clearly see it wasn't, but if that's what I wanted to say, He'd have to write what I told him. I didn't want him to go to jail. I just wanted him to stop. The cop said he had to take me away, as it was the 3rd time I called them, so I packed as much as I could carry. They took me to a place where I had photos taken and told a counselor all about it.

They then took me to a women's refuge. I was there for a few weeks before he found me there. They sent me on a bus back to my parents place. The police testified on my behalf and he was given a DVO. I was pretty messed up for a while. I started drinking and doing more drugs until I met the father of my 2 children. Now 6 and 3 months old.

Sometimes there are triggers with sex, and songs that remind me of my ex. Thankfully my partner is good, and supports me through a lot. My ex rang me when I was in labor with my son and begged me to go back to him. He asked me to name my son after him. I didn't know what to say, so I told him I would. Then after the labor he rang me again, and my mum took my phone off me, and gave him a good piece of her mind, and I have never heard from him since. I'm now studying to be a case manager for DV victims in women refugees.

Survivor: Catherine Percival

* * *

I was four months pregnant when I met what I thought was my prince charming. I was pregnant alone and he knew exactly what I wanted and needed. He treated me like a princess. I thought he was everything I needed and more. Three months in, things started to change. He had heard some news about his ex girlfriend, and started smashing his things up. I tried comforting him and hugging him to settle him down. He then strangled me and took off but that was only the beginning.

I was physically and emotionally abused for months to follow. He beat me at a park, in front of many kids and adults, because I walked away from him being a smart ass. He beat me in his shed throwing me stomach first into the wall while pregnant. I was told I wasn't allowed out without make up on. I was told I was ugly and fat. He even threw me down a flight of stairs 2 weeks before I had baby. I thought I had lost him.

One day, when my son was two months old, I had enough and told him that. Enough was enough, and I didn't want him to be my then fiancée or adopted father to my child. He made me repeat my sentence, and then ran to the kitchen and grabbed the biggest kitchen knife there. He held it to my throat and tried cutting my tattoo off while my son was in my arms. I held him off with all my strength whilst trying to protect my baby. He forced me to suck his dick while he held the knife to me, and my baby was in my arms. He then told me if I was to ever leave not only would he kill me, but my family one by one. I couldn't do that to my son, nor my family. I felt like I had to suck it up and deal with it. I was depressed and just wanted my own life back but was so scared for the outcome if I did go.

Months had gone by with lots of abuse. I eventually found out he had slept with my so called best friend of 14 years. I took off from his place so fast. I was so scared he would catch me. But I left. One night he came to see my son, and I let him. I thought this was the only father my son knew. He started punching and kicking me repeatedly with my baby in my arms. He strangled me that night. I blacked out and came to while he was punching me. He turn around to grab a knife, or gun, I'm not sure what it was, out of his bag. I got up and ran so fast to my neighbors' house.

My son and I were put in a refuge by cops for three months. I got a restraining order, He got jail time, and copped a fine. It has been two years and he still tries to follow me around and chase me. Sometimes I'm still scared to walk out of my front door, wondering what he will do if he ever finds me. There will always be what if's, but I don't let that control me anymore. I'm alive and so is my son. We made it out and I could not be happier.

♛ **Survivor: Monique Alvisse**

* * *

I really don't know where to begin. It was a long journey and one that will forever be within me. I met my ex-husband, father to my son, and adopted father to my daughter, at work. We worked for the same company and were nothing more than friends for years. I ended up leaving that place of employment, getting married, and moving out of town. Upon my divorce, I returned to my parents home and my mother said a man from my old place of employment would call periodically just to check on me, and that he was really nice and cared for me. She said he was disappointed that I had married, and that I should give him a call. We began dating. He was really nice. He brought me flowers, and wrote me cards. I felt like a princess. I really loved the attention. I was impressed that he kept an immaculate house; he even ironed his jeans. We married and when I was pregnant things started to change. First, I found a video of him and his ex-girlfriend having sex. I thought it was a movie, and wow, was I in for a surprise.

    I left and went to my mothers. He came out and I ended up going back home with him. After my son was born, he began hitting me. Once, I had our son in my lap and he jerked me up and our son fell, hitting his head on a coffee table. That night I thought I was going to die. He choked me so hard, I was losing consciousness and all that I can remember was thinking my kids were not going to have a mother. He released his hold just as everything was going black. Adrenaline kicked in and I grabbed the phone and pressed 911 before he got the phone away from me. The police came and I was too afraid to let them arrest him because when I asked the police officers how long they could keep him, they told me honestly he'd be out within the hour most likely. So I didn't want to press charges. I was sure if I did and they let him out, he would definitely kill me.

    At this point, I'd already seen him do horrible things, like shoot an innocent dog. My neck stayed bruised for a very long time. You could actually see exactly where his fingers grasp around my neck. The abuse continued. I got to the point where I felt I couldn't live like that any longer, and I told him I wanted a divorce. He exploded and then calmed down and went out into the woods with a gun, saying he was going to kill himself. I believed him and called the cops. As a result, he voluntarily committed himself into a mental hospital. Each and every time he always ended up getting everyone to believe he was a great person and feel sorry for him. My parents, the counselors and eventually it would be judges he would convince. (He would end up representing himself in court.)

    I hoped the hospital stay helped and I stayed. He got sick and had to be hospitalized with a benign tumor on his lung. While he was hospitalized, I got the mail and realized he had gotten loans from finance companies that charge high interest rates and my name was on the loans. I found out he had gotten his girlfriend (the one in the sex tape) to pose as me when he took out the loans. She signed my name with his on the loans. His girlfriend came to the hospital and I asked her to leave. She left but came back at which time I left. I got some things and went to my moms. When he got out of the hospital, he came out to my moms, and my mom convinced me to let him see our son. (I had been hiding in the bathroom with our son.) She felt sorry for him.

I finally relented and when I went outside, he tried to take my son out of my arms. When I wouldn't give my son to him, he went to his trunk where he'd gotten some of my brothers things that I had left behind because I couldn't get everything when I left. I cherished the little things of my brothers because my brother died in a tragic vehicle accident. They were only things like an ashtray and knickknacks, but he started breaking and tearing them up. He then tried to grab the baby again and I wouldn't release. My poor son, it was like tug of war. He started hitting me and slamming me up against the brick wall, but I held onto my baby. The neighbors happened to see this and called the police. The police arrested him.

I got restraining orders throughout the years, but of course they never worked. Once, he was picked up for violating a restraining order and given a court date and when we got to court, he told the judge I'd been following him, harassing him and calling him on the phone and trying to visit him.. I was astonished! Everything he had been doing to me, he accused me of doing! It was crazy, and the judge ended up chastising me! Things got worse and I didn't have money, a job or really, anywhere to live, because my parents home was seriously just temporary. I was so frightened of him that during the divorce proceedings, I gave him 6 months and I took 6 months custody. I thought it would give me time to get on my feet and I could establish myself and he was appeased because I'd let him have the first 6 months with our son. I honestly felt if I didn't do that he would kill us all. Further, he had threatened that if he was forced to pay child support for my daughter that he'd adopted, he would exercise visitation rights and abuse her. At this point, my parents finally realized how bad he was.

I got a job and rented a rundown trailer and he broke into it several times and cut the phone lines, etc. So, I moved in with a boyfriend. But, I couldn't take being away from my son! It was unbelievably painful! One night I went to his house and begged to be let in and get back with him because I just absolutely couldn't live without my son for six months. Believe it or not, we remarried.

When I finally got to the point I would rather die, than live the life I was living, I finally escaped, but not before he beat me, stripped my clothes off me and took pictures of me shoved into a corner naked. He would beat me into the corner of the bathroom, back up and snap some pictures and I'd try to escape and he'd beat me back again, take more pictures, etc. I went to my mother's again. This is when we discovered he had molested my daughter. She had never told because she said he told her we wouldn't be a family anymore if she told. I think she realized I wasn't ever going back so it was okay to tell. I felt so guilty and I wanted to kill him. My daughters counselor said she was too frail, emotionally to report this to law enforcement. I think they have laws now, wherein this type of thing has to be reported! I got a gun and sat outside his house for a long time. I wanted to kill him. I was overwhelmed with guilt. He never came home that day and I finally left. Of course he has denied he ever touched her.

So, I finally made the break when I got to the point that it was okay to die and death would be better than the life I had. I used to pray that I would just live until my son was eighteen. Once I made this last break, he would acknowledge my son during some Christmases and Birthdays and yet some would pass without an acknowledgment. He would be supposed to pick my son up from school for his weekend and never show and my poor son would be sitting in the principal's office waiting for me to come get him. He belittled my son throughout all these years, telling him he wasn't worthy to breathe the same air as him and things of the sort. Once when my son was a teenager and went to visit him, he had sex with a drug addict and then sent the woman into my sons room.

Throughout the years I have continued to fear for my life. He has done things like try to run over me with his vehicle. I lost a car my parents had given me due to his gambling debts and filing bankruptcy. He has abused all three of us, our son, my daughter and me so many times, I can't even remember them all. I have blocked out so much of it, trying not to remember over the years. Back in the day, when all this was happening to us, there were no laws to protect us like there are today. I had only a high school education and could make just about minimum wage. My daughter ended up living with my parents for several years after our last divorce. I can remember only having enough money for a happy meal for dinner for my son and I wouldn't eat. Just things like that.

I still fear him, but can't let him know. He has continued to threaten my life over the years. I am now 53.

My children will have scars forever because of my poor choices, lack of education, fear. I thank God there are better laws in place for others.

🜲 **Survivor: L. C.**

* * *

I was working at a large office when our firm relocated in late 2003, to a newly constructed building. I noticed this man that I had never seen before and he intrigued me. I saw him constantly in the halls, but did not know who he was. I tried to make small talk with him, but he said that his foreman wouldn't let his employees socialize with our employees. His company had been hired to fix all the damage that had been done by the movers to the expensive wood work throughout the building.

I tried incessantly to find a way to be on the floor that he was working on, to make eye contact, to say hello. After a while I would be able to get him to talk for a few minutes, but that would be it. Several weeks went by and I caught him in the elevator bank, I told him that I was flying to NYC with a friend for the weekend and that he should come with us, my treat. He wasn't able to get a way, but thanked me for the offer and thought maybe we could get together when I got back.

When I got back, the small talk continued and a group of us were going to happy hour. I handed him a piece of paper with my number and told him to either meet us at happy hour or call me. He called and had me meet him at a bar close to his house; we started seeing each other every day after that. We would "accidently run into each other in the elevator, stairwell, parking garage, and would meet after work for happy hour. He drove to work in a nice Durango, which is what he would pick me up in when we went out.

We had gone on dates to decent restaurants and he paid, so I figured he wasn't a slacker, plus I knew he had a job. He had invited me over to his house; a three bedroom split level on a cul-de-sac, so again there were no red flags. We hung out after work, so I didn't spend much time at his house in the beginning.

He started introducing me to his friends and they would all make comments like "you're not his type" "how did you two meet," things that I just brushed off. To me, he was good looking, and I wasn't ugly, so I didn't know what they were referring to, and I never bothered to ask. Instead of happy hour with my co-workers, we would go to happy hour at seedier bars. He liked to shoot pool, and he liked to drink. Every once in a while he would get mad in the bar about something random and want to fight, I would have to force him to leave the bar, and as I had never dated anyone like this, I didn't think anything of it.

The bar situations started to escalate to full on fights…fights where I would drive getaway. Fights where others would drive getaway and I would have to find him. We lived in such a small town that everyone knew who he was and how he would act when provoked. It was always the outsiders that provoked him because he was only 5'8" and they didn't think he was a threat. Again, I didn't think this pertained to me, he wasn't mad at me…I didn't do anything wrong.

Months later when I was emotionally committed, the little flags started to pop up. I found out the Durango was not his, it was his mother's. The house that he lived in was not his, it was his mother's. He had three children that did not live with him, but he saw occasionally, and their mother had a restraining order against him. His mother said that it was bogus, that the children's mother had lied, and because I loved him, I believed it. His job was also a condition of his parole and once off parole, he quit his job.

Once I was the only source of income, his anger turned towards me. He wanted to know my every whereabouts. If I didn't answer the phone fast enough, he accused me of cheating on him. If we were out in public and a stranger asked me a question; he assumed I wanted to sleep with them. He would watch me in public from afar to see what I was doing. He would do the same from my home, parking in the cul-de-sac behind and watching my house. Once when my oldest daughter was lying in bed with me watching TV, she had got up to get something and he thought it was another man and through a pipe wrench through the window.

We went on a camping float trip with two of his younger children. They bus you and your raft or canoe up the river and you float down to the camp site. He drank a fifth of Jack Daniels while we were floating down the river. Once back at the campsite, I was trying to attend to the peed in sleeping bags when he started yelling for me to get him some dry pants. I asked his daughter to get him a pair and he said no, I asked you to get them. He then chased me out of the tent and over to my car and put his fist through the windshield, it looked like a baseball had hit it. When I tried to walk away, he chased me to the middle of the campground and lifted me up by my neck with my feet dangling, yelling at me. All the campers looked on watching; no one stepped in. He remembered nothing the next day and promised to stop drinking.

He showered me with gifts and flowers; to this day I hate orchids. I tried multiple times to leave, but he threatened me and my children. People always say they would never let anyone do that to them, but until you are in the situation, it's hard to say what you would do.

The final incident happened when we went to check on rental property of his mother's in another state. He again had been drinking at a bar; I had learned not to drink so I could better diffuse situations as they arose. We ended back at the house after the bar closed with a friend he ran into at the bar. I was trying to sleep in an empty room on a sleeping bag while he was having a heated conversation with his friend about the incident that sent him to prison. The friend eventually left, leaving me with my boyfriend drunk and enraged.

He started throwing beer bottles in the kitchen; I got up and tried to calm him down. There was a pallet of bricks outside that he began throwing windows and glass in the back door. The bricks bounced off the windows cracking them, but not breaking them, which enraged him more. He threw a brick at the shed window which shattered loudly. I told him we should go inside because he was being too loud. Once inside, he started picking up the refrigerator and throwing it against the kitchen wall. After several throws, the wall was completely destroyed.

I walked out of the house and put the dog in the car and he came after me wanting the keys to my new BWM. I told him no, that he was too drunk to drive; I didn't want him to wreck my car as he had wrecked his BMW twice. He demanded the keys and when I stood my ground he started to chase me down the driveway. I was in pajamas and I lost a flip flop in the chase. He tackled me about fifty feet from the street and had me pinned, he stood over me demanding the keys. He said he was going to rip my face off if I didn't give him the keys. At this point I was in fear of my life, I thought I am going to die in the middle of nowhere in the middle of a corn field.

Then I heard the most wonderful words; "freeze, put your hands in the air." The neighbors did not recognize my car and thought that the house was being robbed and had called the cops. Sadly had it been his car in the driveway, they probably would have ignored the commotion because that is where his last bout of domestic violence took place that was partially why he went to prison.

As we were out of state, I bonded him out and I had to co-sign; he again had no memory of what occurred. He apologized profusely for what he had happened and said he would stop drinking, those famous words. When we got back home, I started distancing myself from him. I wouldn't come over every time he called; I wouldn't stay as long as I usually did when I did go over. He started to notice and left over twenty-one minutes of threatening voicemails between my home phone and cell phone; but we were still quasi together.

We had made plans to go to dinner when I got off work on a Monday. It was taking me a little longer to get home because I stopped to get my dry cleaning, so I was nervous that he was going to be mad. I called his mother to check in with her because he wasn't answering his cell. She said that he had gotten a check in the mail and he was not at home. Any time he got any kind of money, it meant he was at the bar and if he was at the bar from the time the mail came, I had no interest in meeting him for dinner. When he finally called, I told him that he should just hang out with his friends, and call me tomorrow; plus it was snowing. He was a little hesitant, but eventually agreed.

Later that night my phone rang from his land line, he always called from his cell phone so this was odd. When I answered, he was totally incoherent, I couldn't understand anything he was saying other than I needed to come to his house. He had totaled his car and left it in the middle of the road. He wanted me to say that I was with him. I told him that he needed to get help, that I was not getting involved with whatever happened. He needed to get checked into treatment.

A week later he checked into an inpatient rehabilitation center over 1,000 miles away for a six week stay. He was not allowed contact with family for the first few weeks. I flew down to visit with him the week before he was to be discharged and met with the counselors to go over discharge treatment and things that I needed to be aware of for his release. I had full access to everything from that point on at the treatment center.

Two days before his release he started acting weird on the phone. I kept asking him what was going on and he would respond with nothing, why you are asking me that. He also forgot that the cell phone (that he snuck in) was on my plan, so I had access to the voicemail, and when I listened to it I heard the messages with a girl's name. I called the rehabilitation center to see if they could tell me something and they said that he had been kicked out, they couldn't tell me anything further because he had revoked my rights to information. I called him again and asked what was going on, he again said nothing. I asked who the girl was and he wanted to know how I knew. I told him I did not want to see or talk to him when he got back, and called to shut the cell phone off.

When he arrived back on Friday, he started blowing up both my house and cell phone. I called his mother and told her that if he did not stop, I would be an active participant in the case that was still pending in the other state. The calls stopped, but he also jumped bond and went on the run with the girl from rehab. I thought I was in the clear. No calls, no creepy sightings of him in a distance; everything seemed to be going good, except his mother came and stole our dog.

A few months went by and I got a call from the bondsman saying that as he had jumped bail and I was a co-signer, I was responsible for the remainder of the bond. I told him to give me some time to figure out what I could do as I did not have that kind of money. As luck would have it, I started receiving blocked calls from my abuser which I didn't answer. He would leave messages wanting to know if I was going to be on his side if he showed up for court; I continued to avoid the calls. He was extremely persistent, he would call back to back, over and over; then the calls stopped.

A week later I got a call from a number that I didn't recognize, so I answered it. I was a collect call from an inmate at a correctional institution, I accepted. He had been picked up close to the border of Mexico, or so he says, with him you never know what story is true. He again wanted to know if I was going to testify for or against him if he went to court, I told him that I didn't want to have any part of it and he needed to leave me alone. My next call was to the bondsman to let him know where he was to have him extradited back to stand trial, and to get me out of having to pay the bond.

As he had jumped bail, was a flight risk and had several charges for assault on law enforcement officers along with the other charges, he was not given bond. He sat in county for months awaiting trial, constantly calling my house; sometimes collect, sometimes having his mother three-way. His mother would sit outside my house and report to him what I was doing, if there were cars there, if I was home; I finally reported her to the police for harassment.

When he was finally granted $100,000 cash bond, cash, not a bondsman, not putting up collateral, cash; when I heard his family was getting the money together to get him out I panicked. I secretly gave my two weeks' notice at work, packed what I could of my house, found a job out of state and drove over 1,000 miles; but not before I took the dog back.

I settled in to my new job, got a little rental in a crappy part of town and took up shooting guns. I still paid on the house that I owned and money was tight, but I was alive. I followed his case from afar and he ended up not having to do anytime other that the time he had served and one of his conditions was he was to have no contact with me. After about six months in my new home with my new number, I received a phone call from him. I had not given my number out to anyone, I had not told anyone where I went, and to this day I do not know how he got this information.

I started looking into ways to hide and found out that I could change my identity by providing documentation of abuse. I submitted police reports, letters from witnesses, protection order etc. to the Social Security

Administration with hopes that I would be granted a new identity. While going through the process, they explain to you what you are giving up.

You need identification to get anything nowadays, and when you change your identification your past is gone. Your work history, credit history, medical records, birth certificate, it is all gone. If you try to rent a place that needs to do a background check, you have no background. If you try to get a job and they want to call former employers, you have no former employers. If you want to purchase something on credit, no have no credit history. If you were a lawyer or a doctor, you aren't now, you start back at nothing. You cannot get a passport because you don't have a birth certificate under your new identity. You will have trouble proving past abuse because your court papers and medical records are in your old name.

I agreed to it because I was tired of looking over my shoulder, tired of wondering what that noises were, tired of being tired. I submitted all my paperwork and again gave my two week notice. I packed up what I could in a smaller truck, sold my backup car to pay for the move and drove to the other side of the country to start over again. My re-birth happened in 2008, and boy was it a rocky birth. I could not find employment anywhere. After working at such a great job with benefits and a yearly bonus, I had to settle for working retail at $8 an hour. I had to get rid of my BMW because it was tied to the old me; I loved that car.

After eighteen months of backbreaking retail, I decided to go back to school. I completed my associates in a year by attending four schools at once and overloading each semester, then transferred to the university and completed my bachelor's in another eighteen months; all with grants and scholarships. I have done volunteer work with nonprofits in the legal community, received a 40 hour certification in domestic violence awareness, and 40 hour training in mediation.

Today I am happily married housewife, who would love to be working, but due to the economy and the competitiveness in the job market, I am still unemployed.

My advice to anyone dealing with domestic violence is to get out; THINGS can be replaced, LIVES cannot.

Survivor: Jane Frank

* * *

It is easy to get lost in the conflicting emotions that come with stepping over that line drawn in the sand. You can whirl down through grief straight out into joyous freedom and drop all the way back to insecure conditioned doubt. But you have already stepped over the line.

You know that the line is there. You know that one day, one day, one day, one day, this will end. But you don't know how. Will he leave? Will he die? Will he get a job overseas, jet off alone and send money home? Will you win the lottery, keep it secret, and disappear? Will you kill him? Will he try to kill you? and suddenly all the neuroses that he has spawned in you will evaporate and leave Lara Croft brandishing the hand blender like a chainsaw and begging him to make your day?

No. It will be hard and harsh and painful and depressing and wrong. The wrongness will be the most difficult to get past, because this should never have happened. It isn't our fault, but we did let it happen. Working out why is something that will take time and probably talking.

In my case, I dithered behind that line for years. It started with money. With him it was always money that came first, with himself a step behind. He was entitled to be paid for and therefore resented paying for anything. He did, because we were doing the right things and I was at home looking after our children but he made big points of indicating that it was my turn to pay, despite the fact that I only had Child Benefit, for the benefit of my children, to spend. I never saw a penny of the money he earned for our family. We were on holiday in Cornwall when I got the first "Well I paid for" list and was bullied into spending the money for my children's clothes on whatever he had decided I should pay for. He never bought anything that the children needed. That's the first.

Then there was the night that he wished me dead. We were engaged. He had already driven me to a breakdown, although I was still years off working that out. I wasn't truly mentally well but that didn't stop him from telling me frequently how much that inconvenienced him, how much my suicide attempt had harmed him, how useless I was and he had wanted so much more from me. "I wish you would die!" in a drunken rage after a two day drinking binge. That was the death of it but neither of us checked for a pulse. That was the worst.

Two years later (when I had worked hard and alone to recover myself fully and be capable of truly having the future I was meant to have), under the near constant criticism, verbal assault and bitter projection of his insecurities onto me, it came. The line snapped under my feet and was done. His omnipresent verbal abuse, coupled with his incessant gas lighting of my perceptions, feelings and concerns and his constant demands that I think about him, his worries, his perceptions, his (fraudulent) feelings, took flight with his drinking and after two nights and one day of binge drinking, he took it beyond me and gave my daughter a panic attack. And we were done. That was the line, right there. It should have been for me that I stood up and took my rightful place – in control. But it wasn't. I ended the relationship. He went back to the pub.

I locked the door, called the police, called a friend and when he came back and broke into the garage to get a ladder to break into the house he was locked out of, he was arrested. I realized then that I would be fine. I laughed. That was the last.

I laughed a bit more when I found out that he soiled himself when he was arrested. But this didn't stop him. I was clearly terrified but I was finally in control and I could not let go. He was told to leave permanently. He was in shock. I pitied him. He did this. He deserved it. I'm not a horrible person though. If I was then I would never have compromised and obeyed myself into a breakdown and my daughter would never have a panic attack and my son would never had had to tell me to call the police on his father, when he saw him with that ladder. But that's done and here we are.

He has tried every trick in The Narcissist's Handbook. He has blamed me for his behavior, he has harassed me with phone calls and unexpected visits, he has sat and verbally abused me for hours when we were supposed to be sorting out finances, he has messed up all the bills on purpose to create work for me, he has lied to his friends, he has lied to my friends, he has harassed my family and friends, he has tried to paint me crazy, he has denied his actions, he has claimed that his decisions to be nasty and drunken are just, he has manipulated, he has begged, he has gas lighted me, he has tried to dominate. He failed. I went to everyone who would listen and in the end the Freedom Program told me to talk to one specific solicitor. When he started phoning people to tell them I was insane and over-reacting, I called her. She works with Women's Aid. She got me Legal Aid. I have the house, I have the kids, and I pay for it all myself, because I am far more capable than he ever thought me to be. He's alone, renting a room, hoarding his pieces of silver, hated by his children.

The big secret is that strength snowballs. You can be so scared that you are shaking but you can still make that one brave decision. All it takes is to make the decision once and carry it through. There might be no warning, be ready. And know; know so hard that you can feel the bindings, that you are not alone. There is an army waiting to have your back. Call it!

♛ **Survivor: Prometheus Unbound**

* * *

When I was sixteen years old, I met "The Love of my life" or as we will call him "Paddy". He was much older than I, and that being said very mysterious and experienced and very, very intriguing. We kept in contact through Facebook and Gmail. At first we were never anything real, we'd comment on threads on Facebook or send private messages. After a while it became more than comments and innocent 'How are you's' turned into something I'm not very sure any sixteen year old would be ready for. As my parents were divorcing, and my father was gone -all the time-, and my brother and I fighting nonstop, I looked to him for comfort and love I felt I was missing. HE of course always had the right thing to say, and had a way of comforting me that no one ever had. he was handsome, Irish, sweet, caring, creative, and "Loved me to bits" Which, at the time was all I wanted to hear. Little did I know the real story.

The man I was so smitten with was about to turn my whole entire world upside down. Our relationship, as I said, was online and on the phone. For months all I was allowed to do was talk to him. If I was at school, rehearsal, with my friends or family, he was angry. He got defensive and said that if I really Loved him I would choose to talk to him instead of them. Even going to school or work in his mind was pointless and it was a way he thought I was using to get space from him, or to cheat. So, to avoid conflict I started doing everything he asked, I stayed in instead of hanging out, spoke to him on the phone instead of doing my homework or spending time with other people. Video chatted with him instead of going to sleep. Gave him my time instead of my family. He put down ANYONE that was in my life that wasn't him. He made me feel like HE was the only one that was worthy of my time or my Love. When I was seventeen he came to visit me in America. We met up in Good old New Orleans. We were staying in a hotel not too far from Bourbon Street and going out almost every night and having a blast! One not so special day we were just hanging out at a bar there and he was extremely drunk and I wasn't really holding up any better. So that being said he started showing his ass and trying to pull my clothes off in public, started calling me names and pushing me on the ground. The bartenders were trying to help, and the security man as well. A while later we were trying to get a taxi home and he was pushing my head into the window of the cab. Biting my arms and legs. Hitting the cab driver.. and he let us out a bit of a walk from our hotel. "Paddy" Threw my stuff into the street and started climbing a fence to another building's yard. I pulled him down and without missing a beat Paddy balled up his fist and punched me right in the face. I immediately hit the ground and he started to kick me. I curled up in a ball and just took it. He walked away and with tears and shaky legs I tried to get him back to the hotel room. After he was finally there almost an hour and a few more punches later I tried to put him to bed and covered him up leaving him with a kiss goodnight as I tried to sneak out the door. He of course, woke up and I went to his side and asked if he needed anything he rose up and pushed me away calling me names and saying he was going to kill me. Startled I just stood there and he turned and kicked me full force right in the stomach. After a few minutes of him repeating this and other physically violent things the room was left a mess and I was outside looking for help. A young man came to my assistance. Paddy, at this point, is missing in action and I don't care.

The man from room 202 helped me clean the blood off of me from Paddy's.. episode and told me I could stay with him if I needed to. I go outside to look for my boyfriend and he has been causing trouble, Of course. He has a metal bar of some sort and is waving it around and as I try to fight it from him a man from the upper floor asks if I need help, I tell him no and to leave me alone. Shortly after a few more hits from Paddy I find the man standing in front of my with a hammer in his hand. Me, being terrified for my life start to cry and Paddy is egging him on and 202 trying to calm things down.. It was a mess. The man swung the hammer and I stood up blocking my boyfriend (I felt like he was still my partner and I would do whatever I needed to protect him because of that). The man was not going to hurt a poor scrawny young girl with a hammer so he threw it on the ground, took me by the arms and pushed me to the side ordering 202 to put him to bed.

The man wanted to call the cops and I assured him that everything was fine. I should have called my Mother. I should have asked my sister for help. Maybe I should have taken 202 up on his offer, or even the scary man with the hammer. But instead, like a silly teenager, I went back to our room, got into bed, and snuggled into the bed next to a man who had just beaten the shit out of me and threatened both of our lives. The next day he was "Sorry" and said it would never happen again.

But it did. Over, and over, and over. I felt alone. I couldn't tell anyone. Maybe out of embarrassment, or fear they wouldn't believe me. Maybe I just didn't want to believe that this was happening to me. Months of "You wouldn't need to hang out with your friends if I was enough for you" "Your sister can wait.." "If you really loved me.." "College? Why would you go? You can't afford it and you don't need a degree to work at Wal-Mart which is where you want to be right?" And let's not forget the drunken phone calls "I'm fucking all of my girlfriends and they are hotter than you" "You're nothing but an ugly (insert insulting name here)" "You're lucky to have me.." and so on and so forth.

I felt like my life was a movie. Like it was unreal. People don't really speak to other people this way do they? Later on I would learn that it's true, 'humans don't go around destroying other humans.' Despite all of this and more I saved all of my money and flew to Ireland to see him. The first few weeks were great.. Despite him snooping on my Facebook, jealous of me massaging my twin brother and best friend. Oh and let's not forget all the fuck buddies I got to meet. And yes I met them all, became friends with them and even got close just to be told later on that he had cheated on me with almost all of the women and YOUNG girls that I met and befriended.

After a few weeks, a few hard drugs, and a lot of drinking and he's back to hitting me again. All of the time. I had no family. No friends. I felt so alone. There were so many days that I wished I could just curl up and die. Or go back in time and maybe date that guy from theatre or history.. They seemed nice... Certainly they would never lay a hand on me.

Paddy got what he wanted I wasn't allowed to speak to my family. My friends. My co workers. Could only eat certain things at certain times. And let's not even get into the terrifying "Intimate" side of things. It was all around terrible. I was stood up on my wedding day (really a blessing). I was being belittled every day. I was never good enough.

One day it got bad again. Very bad.. So bad I hid in my own home until he was gone. So... I flew home. Home, where I had a 'family' A broken family but a family. Home where I had friends and a support system. Where people loved me and saw a light in my eyes. Where people seemed to really enjoy me. Where I didn't have to be afraid of being hit. Or abused in any way. I was finally safe.

It was the hardest and easiest thing I have ever done. Hard because I truly had feelings for this man. Easy because I could see a light that I hadn't known before.

This man no longer is a part of my life and I'm happier than ever! I do have a new boyfriend now and he is more than I could ask for! He was with me though a horrible battle with cancer, that I won! I absolutely adore him.. And we do at times... Not exactly get along.. but who doesn't do that? He is a huge part of my life and I couldn't see my life without him OR his precious daughter. My life is worth living, and I AM more than, silly Paddy, ever told me I was. And boy, was he wrong about me.

♛ **Survivor: J. B.**

* * *

I met my husband when I was 21. He was 32. He was charming and loving and knew all the right things to say. We were dating for a month before I got pregnant with our daughter. That's when the emotional abuse started.

I thought about leaving him then, but he always guilted me into staying. "Our child needs both of her parents" he would say. "I love you and I'll change" were his favorite words to use to manipulate me. I was 21. What did I know?

Fast forward 10 years. I stayed, we married and built a life together. It was a life of constant belittling, control and manipulation. But we were together and a family and that's what was important, right?

I finally had enough when one day I woke up and realized how truly miserable our life was together. How I always felt bad, and sad, and angry. I was never happy anymore. Ever. I decided it was time to go.

It took me months to plan my exit. I'm lucky and have a supportive family and was able to move home. I moved out in September of 2013. Everything went smoothly in the beginning. We were more civil to each other then we had been in years. We were sharing custody of our daughter without a court order. Everything was going great until a month later on Halloween.

Below is what happened next. This is my victim impact statement to the judge who handled my case.

Dear Judge Haendiges:

On October 31, 2013, mine and my daughter Serena's life were changed forever.

That afternoon I was on my way to pick Serena up from school when I received a text from the defendant, Kenneth Markle, saying that she was not at school. He stated that she had missed the bus that morning so he had kept her home. I sent a text back saying that I was on my way to his house then to get her because we had trick-or-treating plans with a friend of hers. The defendant then informed me that they were not home (this was a lie) and not to go into his house.

For the next 3 hours I sat in my car in front of his home waiting for them to return. The defendant continued to text with me but would not answer his phone when I called. When I asked where they were and if I could come and get them both, I was either ignored or told that they were on their way. Shortly after 6pm, I noticed the downstairs neighbor leaving and at that point

I received a text from the defendant that I could enter his home to retrieve Serena's book bag. He said that since I was in such a hurry that I should get her bag and they would be there shortly. I continued to wait, not feeling comfortable entering his home without him there. At this point it was already getting dark outside. After another 15 minutes, I received another text from the defendant saying to grab her bag from the hallway and they would be there any minute. It was at this point that I decided to enter his home.

I unlocked the door with my key and noted right away that the hallway was dark. I tried to turn on the lights with the light switch, but they didn't go on. (I found out later that the defendant had covered the only window in the hallway with a dark towel and had taken all of the light bulbs out of the sockets.) I went up the first set of stairs to the landing and bent to look on the floor for Serena's bag. As I was bent over I was struck on the top of my head, hard. My vision blurred and I saw stars. (I firmly believe that the defendant was aiming for my face and would have succeeded had I not been bent over.) At that point I straightened up and turned to look up the hallway and that was when the defendant struck me again on the left side of my head. When my vision cleared a bit from the second strike, I saw the defendant coming at me again with a baseball bat in his hands. This time I was able throw myself back against the wall to avoid another blow. The defendant then dropped the bat and came at me with his hands. At first he tried to put me in a headlock but I was able to struggle just enough to keep him from getting the grip he needed. He repeatedly tried to smash my face into the stairs while grabbing handfuls of my hair. During the struggle we ended up at the bottom of the stairs, me on my back, and the defendant kneeling on my chest with both of his hands around my neck strangling me. He kept repeating "You ruined my family" over and over again. It was at this point that I came extremely close to losing consciousness.

The next thing I remember is hearing my daughter's frantic cries. This snapped me back into reality. Whether she knows it or not, Serena saved my life at that moment. She was screaming at the defendant "Dad what are you doing? Stop!". The defendant looked up at her and very calmly told her "Go back upstairs. Everything is going to be okay now". Serena continued to scream at him to stop as I begged for my life. Finally he released his hold on my throat and ran up the stairs while I threw myself out of the front door. As soon as I was outside I turned to make sure the defendant hadn't followed me and I saw Serena still standing on the landing. I opened the door and grabbed her hand and told her we had to leave. She was only wearing a bra and underwear and said "but mom, I don't have any shoes on". It broke my heart to wrench her out of the house into a cold rainy night in only her undergarments and me covered in blood. We ran across the street to a neighbor's house where the Lackawanna Police were called. I was then transported by ambulance to ECMC. The defendant, with a shotgun in hand, entered into a 4 hour standoff with the Lackawanna Police Department.

As a direct result of this attack I suffered from a concussion, a sprained wrist and ankle, and multiple deep bruises covering most of my body. I also had staples in the top of my head where the initial blow landed and stitches in my upper lip where he smashed my face into the steps. As a direct result of the head trauma I still suffer from debilitating headaches, confusion, and forgetfulness. I find it extremely difficult to concentrate on one task for long periods of time and I get overwhelmed very easily. I also suffer from vivid nightmares that result in waking in a panicked state on an almost nightly basis. None of these things were an issue before the attack.

Judge Haendiges, I would like to ask the court for the maximum sentence that this crime allows. This was an incredibly cowardice act that was well planned in advance and executed with brutal efficiency. It was only due to my daughter's screams and a lot of luck that I was able to walk out of that hall way with my life. The defendant spent that day telling my then 8 year old daughter how he wanted to kill her mother. For her to then walk in on her father strangling her mother who was covered in blood has had a profound effect on Serena. How is a child supposed to deal with this when I as an adult am struggling to do so? While we are both in counseling, I am positive that this experience will haunt us both in some way for the rest of our lives. Not only did I lose myself that day, but Serena lost her mother as she knew her and her father as well. It is going to be a very long road for us both as we struggle to rebuild a new life. It will take quite some time before either of us feels safe and begins to trust again.

He plead guilty to felony assault w/weapon and received the maximum sentence, 7 years in jail and 3 years of probation after the fact. My daughter and I have a restraining order until 2028.

♛ **Survivor: Laura Markle**

* * *

    I met my abuser six years ago. I managed a bar and the owner hired him for security. I didn't like him at first, but eventually we got closer and started dating. I never saw anything different until about six months into the relationship. First time he got mad about something and went to punch my microwave. I pushed him so that he didn't damage something of mine. He looked me in the eyes and said 'Just so you know, if you touch me, you better be ready for what comes your way'. I took off running for the bedroom. He punched and broke my T.V. on the way to chase me in there. He busted the door in, and dragged me to the hallway, where he knocked me down and stood over me punching me and kicking me. I was in total shock because this had never happened with anyone before. I let it go thinking that it was just off behavior, and that it wouldn't happen again.

    Over the next few years there had been a few more times, and I just kind of just got over them as well. I ended up pregnant in 2011 and I was 38. I was shocked and cried for 3 days. Mostly because I knew I was stuck. While I was pregnant he gave me an STD and I thought I was going to lose the baby at 18 weeks. That started a whole path of physical, mental and emotional abuse. He also cheating on me. After I had her he had an affair for over a year and a half. I kept catching him, and every time I did, he would be physically abusive, but I still stayed.

    On Father's day 2012 he tried to kill the girl because she told me he was cheating with her. He was charged with assault with intent to commit murder. She was doing the whole court thing until the end and she didn't show up because he got in her head and threatened her. The case was dropped.

    I thought he was changed and he told me so, I married him in February 2013. In June 2013 we had gotten in a fight and he was all nice and told me to come over and talk. I went over and I knew as soon as I got there I needed to leave. He tried to get the keys from me and I wouldn't let them go. He bit my hand 5 times so hard that it fractured my hand - but I never let the keys go. As soon as he let loose I ran and got away. The worst time that changed my life was March 2014. He accused me of having an affair. He came over and punched, slapped, kicked, threw things at me and stabbed me. He was trying to kill me. He busted up so many walls and things in my house. Luckily his cousin happened to come over to borrow money from me, and saved my life. I wouldn't be here today if it wasn't for him. He got me fired from my job because he threatened people at my work, I lost my house and my car. I took my kids and went to a shelter. Come to find out - he was the one having the affair from 3 months after we got married to a year later when I caught him.

I have a masters in psychology. Always made great money and I am proof that domestic violence can ruin your life or kill you and the only way to get out of it is to leave - it can happen to anyone on any walk of life. He NEVER had any regrets at all - he only cared about who saw it happening. He is Jamaican and killing is a way of life there. He spent 2 tours in Iraq front lines and who knows what he did there to people. Killing me would have been too easy. He always said he was going to kill himself, and I made sure he never had our daughter, because he would have killed her too knowing THAT would kill me. He is a true definition of a narcissist. I was always a stupid bitch and did nothing for him.

After I left and was in the shelter I got to see his whole background and he had 3 major domestic charges and all were dropped because he either threatened them or apologized to the girls, and they didn't pursue it. The next person he is with, will be dead. Prosecutors, judges and officers all over this city want him so bad because he is a loose cannon. I have since filed a PPO and divorce papers. I have put my daughter in a daycare he doesn't know where it is.

I am FINALLY rebuilding my life piece by piece. Therapy at my shelter has helped a lot. I finally got a new job and started last week. I am in the process of new housing and should be moved in a few weeks. I am still trying to get transportation because that has been my hardest struggle, getting around. The story I told above is really just a piece of what I went through. I have started to go back and blog month by month from the day we met in 2009. He put me through hell. I remember some nights just staring at him and wondering how I could get rid of him. I also knew that I was at the point that the next time he touched me, that it was either going to be he or I that didn't make it. I was ready to die or ready to kill. When you are at that point - you are worn down and done!!! 2 days after he almost killed me - we were in the car together and I was driving. He said I want to punch you so bad right now - I said do it. All I ask is that you don't kill me in front of the kids. And I meant it. It is sad when that is what becomes of your life if you stay.

After months of being away, therapy and working on everything I need to do....I am like a new person!!! I have a smile on my face again. I am laughing and actually enjoying life a little bit. I still have some major things to work on and get back on track, but I am away from someone torturing me and having affairs, and that makes all the difference in the world. I have become a huge support for others in the shelter on where to find resources and what doors to knock down to get assistance to have a life again. I was so lucky because I called 2 shelters before this one and they couldn't help me. The first one was for families and not domestic and had no security in place. The second had him listed 5 times as an abuser for other people and they worried about my safety. The one they sent me too is the one I am at now and it isn't a typical shelter - we have our own apartments so it feels like in some way you have a life still. The only problem is their focus is not homelessness or employment - purely domestic and stalking services so you have to research yourself. I did to anyone that would listen and people saw me fighting hard and helped me. I am not a super religious person but I know that the lord took everything away from me for a reason - he knows I was not getting it - and I wouldn't make it the next time and had to wipe out my life. I'm am doing better now and I lost many things, but i have regained my life, and that is what truly matters the most to me.

🏺 **Survivor: Teri Lyn**

* * *

I grew up in a wonderful home with a loving mother and father. As a child I was not exposed to domestic violence. My mother had been married previously and I overheard a conversation with my father about how he wasn't as hard on me as he was my brother. My father told her because I never had the experience that my brother had there was no need to do anything other than change the tone of his voice. I am grateful today for knowing that.

The man I was married to for 18 years, I met as a young woman of 18. He was shy and had beautiful blue eyes. I thought he was more thoughtful than others because he could tell me everything that was wrong in jobs he had done. Most people would do the work and leave it there. His self esteem was low but he was very charming. I was the receiver of a lot of attention and praise. He never dreamed he could ever get anyone like me, and said it would only last a couple of weeks. I asked him to stop buying me a single long stemmed rose regularly because he needed the money to live on. Before I knew it I was taking him out for meals because he had no money.

My mother saw him long before I did and thought he was adorable. Initially she told me he was a gift from heaven. One night I spoke to his stepfather on the phone. I was shocked. Every other word was fuck, and my abuser told me that if I met him he would probably slap me on the ass so don't get offended. That is just the way he is. I had heard the stories about the stepfather and things he had done but had no idea the impact on the child who would become this man. It was only a short time after that the stepfather passed away. My father gave my abuser the money for a round trip ticket. I knew I was in trouble because the week he was gone I was physically ill being away from him. From the first date we became inseparable. I was in love and he was undermining even then.

When the abuser came back from the funeral he cried to me 'Will his stepfather know he loved him?'. Then the stories of all the bad things his stepfather did came pouring out. After all that he told me, he said he did not want to be like his stepfather and worried that he would be. I asked him if he knew it was wrong and he said yes. I told him then you have the power to chose to be different. He advised me that if I married him I should keep the kids safe and run with them if I had to so they would not grow up how he did. He said, "Do whatever it takes." I thought he didn't want to be that way so he could chose.

I had been concerned over my car and had it at a repair shop. The mechanic could find nothing wrong with my car. One evening he followed me to his home ... I wrecked the car on the way, and noticed my abuser did not follow me and I was upset with him. (It's important to know that my oldest brother was killed in a car accident at 17.) I went to my parents, and when I came in the door, I was not hugged by my loving father. I was instead told that he knew I would do something stupid. My focus shifted from being upset with my abuser, to being upset with my father. The phone rang and he asked me where I was. My abuser came and got me. My mother wasn't home. When I came home later she was worried sick about me.

My father had decided he had enough of my mothers complaining about two months after and took my things and put them out on an old picnic table where my abuser lived saying, "If you want her you can have her." I was so stubborn I stayed and when my abuser wanted to go home to California I told him I wanted to go too. He was going to send for me, and I let him know if I went back home, I wouldn't be going anywhere. Before I left Texas to move to California with him, she told me if I were to marry him she would never see her grandchildren. I was a young naive rebellious teen, who wanted to conquer the world. I had been safe growing up so I knew nothing different. So off to California, without saying goodbye, I went.

Upon arrival in California my future mother in law was having her house snaked due to backed up plumbing. The plumber had rented a snake insufficient for the job and it was stuck in the drain somewhere and he wanted her to pay extra for it. There was a garage sale going on, to sell the dead husbands things, and she was an emotional wreck. I had no idea that a letter from my mother had preceded my arrival and it was filled with lies so she was worried about the person I would be. My mother later called and apologized and then my future mother in law told me about the letter.

Not growing up around abuse or seeing it, I was in shock ... One night the family verbally assaulted me in the garage, and I drove my car around the corner and parked. I cried I wanted to go home so bad at that very moment. Boundaries were being violated and I didn't know how to cope with it all. I was only 20 at this point. Nothing was ever discussed with my mother because I didn't want her to hate the man I loved, any more than she already did. She sent a book to me, "Women who love too much", and I threw it in the trash.

In 1988 he finally asked me to marry him. Nobody from my family came for the wedding. It was as if I had been cut off from the world. My abuser had called and spoke to my father, and when he got off the phone he said, "I wonder what he thinks now that I am buying the cow?" I didn't get it before how he would build something up and make you feel great, just to burst the bubble for the emotion, control or defeat. Things went really fast we got a place, first new car, married, and then he started a business. In 1992 our first child was born.

Before she was born I had been out on disability due to an injury and surgery on my ankle. My abuser had been cruel to me about my pain and undermined my attempts to get a job. There would be comments about how I was 'always something'. One night he brought me the gun and bullets and said, " You had better keep these or I am liable to use it." This was after he had taken a tree stump coffee table and thrown it across the living room and busted his bong. I did not smoke marijuana or use drugs but he had ever since I knew him. He could hide and then he stopped trying to. I still loved him but wasn't afraid of him yet. I was definitely confused.

On one occasion he decided he wanted a new car and his truck was almost paid off. I loved his monster truck. He called me from the dealership and said if I didn't get down there and sign the papers too (I had better credit) he would divorce me. I went and signed. Within days the transmission went out and the dealership told him it was the way he was driving and he said it was the transmission. My abuser had the car for less than 6 months since he lost his job. Somehow he talked his brother into it and got out from under it.

When I had our first child I was in heaven. He wasn't around to help and one night he decided to hold her. It was wicked. I stopped him from doing it but he was taking delight in plugging her nose and watching her mouth open. Then he went to hold her mouth shut. I screamed at him and he laughed. My girlfriends took me out for a night and told him he gets to take care of his child for an evening. I went to Mystere at Santa Monica. I love Cirque Du Soleil! What an amazing experience. I came home to a man who refused to change a poopy diaper and a really bad rash on her bottom. My abuser made them suffer for my joy.

Eventually my friends stopped coming around. One told me he is toxic to me. Another didn't come around because his car would be home but he wasn't. I found out he had been having an affair less than 3 months into the marriage with a girlfriend of mine down the street.

Our second daughter was born two years later and after the earthquake. I had gone to Texas to visit my father and wanted to leave. My father explained that he is the father of my children and has rights. I realized my father was a non supportive alcoholic and I had nowhere to turn. My abuser thought I wasn't coming back because he knew he had been a real jerk. Everyday he called to say he was sorry and things would be different. The contractors were making our home better so I could have the kitchen I want, and to just come back. My mother had passed away in 1988 and I really wished she had been around at this point. Her death changed my father forever. I went back to California, and put on a happy face because he had rights and access to money through a family who would readily help him attack me.

I had to had surgery on my nose due to chronic sinus infections. I had a deviated septum, nasal polyps and something else. I left a note with the information of where to pick me up after my day surgery when he got off work. My girlfriend had dropped me off at the hospital. When 6:30 PM rolled around and he still wasn't there I called. My abuser had forgot and I didn't leave a note? I was concerned about my little girls knocking my nose and hurting it but my abuser was horsing around and "accidentally " hit it. He said sorry and started laughing.

We moved to a better home on a busy street in a nice neighborhood. I made a lot of friends and became licensed for a daycare. I never opened it. Instead I volunteered all the while receiving harsh remarks from him about how I need to make money. I was offered a job with the city through volunteering and took it. My first day the car had been "stolen". My mother in law came to the rescue with her car. I found out about 6 months later he had my car stolen. My abuser really didn't want me to be out from under his thumb.

In August right after moving into the new home, we went on a family cruise. All of his siblings and their children. My abuser decided to whip our oldest repeatedly with a belt, because she wouldn't hold my hand and ran away from me and into traffic, on the Cayman Islands. It was a huge topic and the whole family came down on him and forgot about it after another incident with a teenager smoking weed in Jamaica.

I became pregnant and worked up until the last month of pregnancy. The day I was supposed to come home in 1999 after giving birth to another daughter he left me at the hospital until 6 PM. The doctors had been treating me all along as a single mother giving me extra samples because they all saw who he was.

On December 25th 1999 my father took his life. He hadn't been alive since my mother passed away. She was his world. He had called and said to me on Christmas Eve, "I don't know what happened to that light you had, but I sure do miss it." I was outside when the phone rang and did not hear, but I knew my daddy was gone. My father in law came to tell me the news and hugged me while I cried. My father in law was the one person who understood. My abuser came home and congratulated me on being an orphan. After that the abuse escalated.

One night I was talking to a friend, telling them that I wanted to leave the situation and they were telling me he just didn't know how to show his love. He walked up behind me and I didn't hear him. I was accused of cheating and he trashed the home. Broke the front door. Disconnected me from the world so I could not call anyone and cancelled the internet so I lost all my friends emails. That night he tore my clothes, raped me, then held a gun to my head. I heard little footsteps in the hallway and prayed. She quietly turned around and went back to her room. The next morning she asked me why daddy had a gun to my head, and I told her that was a bad dream she had. He then sought out counseling to help me, as he was concerned about my mental state due to the loss of my father. The therapist, like all the others, told me I was fine and to protect myself. This was the first time I ever thought maybe I am in a domestic violence relationship, and then pride stepped in, and said no you're not. I closed the yellow pages after I saw Haven Hills. I did not go.

I was a Girl Scout Leader and it was a father daughter dance. He refused to take the girls, and I said fine stay home and watch the baby. I knew other fathers who would dance with my girls and so would I. That night somebody told me he was outside looking in windows. He had left the baby alone in the house to come and stalk me. I was accused of cheating on him because I was talking to men.

In 2001 we sold our house and had another lined up. He offered to give me half and we go our separate ways. I told him we had far too much history and things were coming together. Lets get counseling and raise the kids. I love you. He paused a moment then said, "It's a good damn thing you said that. I would bankrupt my business so you won't see a dime. I will exhaust my mother's fortune so you never see your kids. Hell, you'll be lucky to get out alive." Then he left the room laughing.

Our new home was in a new neighborhood in a cul de sac. He was tired of my friends coming over all the time. He tried to isolate all of us. My kids didn't see their friends and he didn't have any. My daughters were bullied at the new school and he was not a loving father. Not a good mix for a child. No support from anywhere and nobody really understood. Even friends who he scared and intimidated didn't understand. I had more friends that said they couldn't hang out because they didn't like how he treated me. If I said anything to him, he wanted their number so he could talk to them. I never gave the numbers up. He was still cheating on me and undermining. He refused to help with anything and trash talked me to everyone who would listen. Nobody even knew I had a job for years because he told them all I was a stay at home mom.

I saw the signs in my children, and I still didn't completely have my head wrapped around it. He would tell them how they would never amount to anything. Lecture them on respect demanding it as he never gave anyone any. One day he came in the house with trash cans, threatening that the house could go in the dumpster, there was so much shit. He said, "You don't get to win!" I yelled back. I found my voice and drug my arm across a shelf full of brand new dishes. That was a horrific experience all together. He had wanted fine china because he deserved it. I finally got him talked into everyday dishes. Fine china to eat on everyday with kids and our lifestyle and his lack of caring for anything made no sense. So I watched the under $30 in dishes fly across the kitchen. The children had already left and hid because of his yelling. I screamed, "You still don't get it. If I don't win, you don't win, we lose. If you don't win, I don't win, we lose. We are all in this together. Either we all win or we all lose." He threw away my daughters favorite stuffed animals and poured grease on them so they couldn't be salvaged.

When the police were called on one incident they told him how to hit the girls so it would not leave a mark. Shortly after there was repercussions for calling the police. He said, "I get to discipline my daughter and you can't stop me. If you try you will not see tomorrow or any other day!" That night he broke her spirit. I reached out to therapists but did not understand that I needed ones that specialized in domestic violence. They all said protect yourself and nobody ever turned him in.

I prayed he would leave me because he had already told me he would kill me if I ever left. He said, "I will hunt you down and kill you. Make no mistake, if I can't have you nobody will." He also said, "The day I have to pay you a dime you are dead." He moved out to be with the woman I thought was my friend. My abuser had been having an affair with her, and I blessed her because I know who she caught. Sadly she had only known abusive relationships. Within a month of him being out, I was told he had her thong panties in a drawer in his bedroom. My abuser would show up with a horrible hangover to watch the kids and we would all leave as he slept it off. He left in January 2013.

There are far too many incidents to list them all. He left our oldest on a busy street, and she was in 5th grade. Neglect was a big one. I begged the youngest to drop her pants at school and show the nurse welts on her from the belt her father used that morning and she refused. Child Protective Services had first been brought in because of the oldest. They asked is he out. I said yes, and they said great job keep him out. They would not get involved later because the complaints needed to come from the kids and not me. Child Protective Services dropped the cases because he started pointing back at me, and they saw me getting them the help they needed, and no issues in the home. I was finally going to Haven Hills, The Jewish Federation Against Domestic Violence, and Valley Trauma Center.

The judge told me to stop going to Al-Anon which I later found out is against the Supreme Court. I kept going. I learned a lot but I could not stop the destruction. I was proud of my girls the day they all spoke up at an LAUSD School Board Hearing, and told their story of how abusive he is. The leader at that meeting said she didn't care. Every professional was there and nobody did anything. The minors council was colluding with my ex according to the Devonshire Police Night Watchman that I spoke with. The police that came and removed the children from the home kept saying, "I don't understand? This is a good home? Why are we doing this?" I appreciate him. He was there in the school board hearing. Nobody was there for me as I watched them take my babies away. They were sent to three different homes in three different states and didn't even have each other. Nobody wanted to know their story, or wanted to understand it. The older two had no more counseling and the college classes that my oldest had just started were cancelled..

Things escalated after that. This is a man who would suffocate me with a pillow in my sleep. He kept vandalizing my car, stalking and trying to run me off canyon roads. Nobody did anything. Victims of Crime helped me relocate. After I did I became homeless as I didn't get a job right away. It was a small town with a 14% unemployment rate and nobody knew me. When I took a minimum wage job, and no guarantee of hours while on food stamps he was awarded child support. $357 was garnished from my wages and I earned a whopping $9800 for the entire year. He makes over $100,000 a year after bankrupting that business. I am still paying and so are they.

I finally landed in a neat little town that has AWARE CENTRAL TEXAS in it and a program called WINGS to help others. I am committed to change and get to make a difference. I have been a general manager of a store and in sales. The latest discovery is that my commissions will not be seen as they will go to pay the back owed child support.

Despite it all I know that I am out. This is the last of it and he still has to wake up to himself every day. I am sorry I have missed out on things with my girls for all of this but I had to save us, as nobody else would. I am my knight in shining armor! I pray a car will come into my life. The one I have has seen better days. It's frustrating how they use the legal system against us. People wonder why we stay . I wish I had left sooner, I might have been able to escape with my girls.

My dad said it best, "He has rights." He has the right to abuse everything good as the legal system fails to stop it and turns its back. There is one thing he cannot steal. I will never let him steal my joy. That is the light my dad was missing. Never let them steal your joy. Remember that this too shall pass and there is something great in store for you in the future. All you have to do is believe!

🏵 **Survivor: Freeda Knight**

* * *

I've often said, "Knowing when to walk away is wisdom, being able to is courage & walking away with our head held high is dignity & grace."

Domestic violence crosses all socio-economic lines, and ever growing statistics reveal that in our culture it is 'reported' to occur in one in four American households. Still, many others among us suffer in silence, with no voice. We see the faces of the statistics all around us, as we see shadows of the pain & suffering of our: Mothers (Fathers), sisters (brothers), daughters (sons), friends & neighbors. We've become mindlessly conditioned to think nothing of turning a blind eye. While, many suffer in deafening, resonant silence, lost in a sea of hopeless despair, with no reprieve, and nowhere to turn. Bruises heal, bones mend, but seeds of indignation & paralyzing fear are deeply planted through emotional abuse & grow for a lifetime. Counselors seemed to have empathy & compassion but lacked perspective. So, in hopes of finding peace, freedom from the chains that bound me to my own generational cycle of abuse. And, in a desperate attempt to find, my direction, my way out of the darkness, (that seemed my destined fate), I chose to study Behavioral and Clinical Psychology. I did not have the educational advantages of some of my contemporaries, but I had a library card. So, I crawled into a library, and you might say that I didn't emerge until I had a rudimentary understanding of preprogramming & Classical/Operant social conditioning.

I was 6 years old when I watched, (with my own eyes), my brand new 'Step father' take my Mother's life. Mary Louise Gadberry (25), draw her last breath as her life was senselessly stolen at the hands of domestic violence. Her life was officially relegated to being just another nameless, faceless statistic. The official cause listed on her death certificate reads - "Asphyxiation by strangulation." When I'm alone at night, the memory of watching her struggle, gasp for her last breath, and the color leaving her face haunts me still today, (more than 40 years later.) When I sleep, my eyes still don't close all the way and others tell me that they see the whites while I sleep. And, I still leave a light on because I must be ready to escape at a moment's notice.

After my Mother's murder, I was sent back to live with the man known as my father. Biologically, he really was my father, but he was not like any father that I had ever seen or heard about. He was a jaded, cynical, bitter man, angry at the world, known for his short fuse, blind dissociative rages, making excuses, and never taking responsibility for his reactive behavior. He chose a life of hide and seek from the faces and demons who had taken up residence in his own mirror, rendering him. Going through the motions of 'living' in a prison of his own making.

I recall as early as 5 years old how many nights he would quietly creep into my bedroom on his hands & knees, pulling the cover off of me and taking me from my bed. When my dearest Great Grandmother, (79 at the time), I would hear the creek of the door, and she'd whisper, "Just lay real still honey. Pretend you're asleep & maybe he'll go just on." Until puberty, that rarely was the case. I recall him often stating, "I feed you, give you a roof, and buy you clothes because the law says that I have to. That's more than a lot of kids get. You should be grateful, and earn your keep." With my childhood stolen by a thief in the night, I was numb, hypersensitive and by the age of 6, a generational cycle of domestic violence was already set in motion for me. The seeds of hopeless despair through social acceptability were already deeply planted in the fertile soil of my adolescent psyche. In order to process my reality, and as a learned mechanism of coping and survival, dissociating was the only way to get through it. After all, this could not be happening to me.

At 5 and 6, this man would beat me so severely with a belt, razor strap, toaster cord or whatever was handy. So badly that I had open wounds. I was unable to attend school for fear that someone might discover our dirty family secrets. My G/Grand would stand at the stove weeping uncontrollably as she broke yellow sulfur pellets to make salve to apply to my open wounds to stave off infection. I'll never forget, the stench of the sulfur as it cooked, how it burned as she applied it to my back, how I had to put my face into a pillow to keep from screaming and making too much noise or how my nightgowns / sheets had to be peeled off me the next morning.

By 13, I had outlived my usefulness. He pushed me down a flight of stairs and told me that I would have to go. By 13, I was washed up abandoned and disposed of, seemingly destined to fall through the proverbial cracks.

In my 20s and 30s, broken and alone with no family, I soaked in self pity, empowered/ validated my own anger, as I drowned in dissociative sea of hopeless despair, seemingly destined to fall through the cracks, and become merely just another unfortunate forgotten, faceless statistic, as my Mother had been. As learned mechanisms of survival, I practiced what I'd learned by watching adults, avoidance, hide & seek from myself, and the demons who, by then, had homesteaded residence in my own mirror. In order to insure that the cycle ended with me, despite societal judgment, I felt that I had a moral responsibility to make the executive decision not to have children of my own. In an attempt to find a lifeline and understand myself and my predisposed patterns, I studied tirelessly. It took decades of dissociation playing hide & seek from the child and lady who lived in my mirror.

Being run down by a car by an abuser and literally learning to walk again, having many surgeries, including having had my face rebuilt, my teeth knocked out, as I crawled on eggshells from one bad relationship to another, before I truly understood how, or why my own self deprecating, emotionally masochistic penchant toward domestic violence was pre-programmed. It was my familiar, what I knew. And, not surprisingly, I'd learned to equate control and abuse with love. And, by turning a blind eye, while sweeping it under the rug, society had sent the clear, undeniable message that Domestic Violence was my birthright. "The luck of the draw." And, that I didn't deserve anything different.

As a mechanism of survival, I've walked on enough eggshells, learned the patterns of the predators and what to watch for from a very young age. With no family, I went from one abusive relationship to the next, predator after predator. In retrospect, it was just a matter of time before an attempt on my own life was made.

So far, I've been: burned, beaten, controlled, literally starved to the point of being hospitalized, watched others enjoy a Christmas dinner while I gave thanks for my peanut butter sandwich. One abuser even stuck a needle in my arm, and loaned me out to a friend. So, not being blessed with a family or a built in support system, I was slated to fall through the cracks. And, I did for years and years. I was programmed and conditioned to go through the motions. You see, I never learned how to LIVE. An enslaved life of domestic violence was all I'd ever known.

Countless failed attempts at relationships proved that that attitude only served to affect me to react out of a place of desperation, fulfilling my own self defeating prophecy. Now, disabled by domestic violence, life seemed hopeless as I was financially forced to reply on predators with divisive controlling agendas as they lined up, one after another, to feed from my desperation under the guise of 'rescuing me', as it seemed that I was forced, day by day, to allow them to chip away pieces of my soul. I couldn't understand as I watched respectable people systematically turn a blind eye to my bruises and suffering, control through starvation, for fear of getting involved.

It was clear to me that even many of those respectable people were souls lost in a sea of darkness, playing an exhausting, perpetual game of hide and seek from themselves (their own soul.) Many hiding beneath the walls of fear through judgmental programming mindlessly 'conditioned' to accept empty platitudes of empty polite social affectation, proprietary sensibilities, being decently, politely hypocritical, socially acceptable levels of dissociation, reactive anxiety based anger and insanity, as the social norm. As a direct lateral result, I see many, like myself systematically fulfilling self defeating prophecies, yet unable to understand why we find ourselves perpetually trapped in self deprecating vortexes of malcontented unhappiness, in self imposed prisons, built by walls of self protection through the detrimentally programmed reactionary mechanisms of survival.

Fast forward to 2003. My face was sliced and diced. I was intentionally run down by a car. I literally crawled when I couldn't walk and to date, it has taken 8 surgeries, relearning to walk/feed myself. I tell people, it takes a bathtub full of 'Elmer's' & bunch of Popsicle sticks to put 'Humpty Dumpty' back together again." Now, I am disabled from Domestic violence. People say, "I'm sorry to hear of your accident." I reply, 'Thank you, that's very kind of you to say'. But it was no accident. It really is true what they say, "the apple doesn't fall far from the tree."

After I was hit by a car, I had nowhere to go to heal. A 92 year old Hopi Elder taught me HOW to live. These days, I treasure every day that I have on this Earth and the empathy and compassion that rose from the ashes of my suffering. It is a gift. I think of it as my superpower that I use to help others find freedom, from the blind bondage of their enslaved existence.

I now live on very limited means. And, I often find myself at 'the Crossroads', forced to choose between life sustaining independence or insurance. No human should ever be forced to make that choice. So, in order to have a roof over my head, just as I was programmed to do, I'm forced to acquiesce to the agendas of control through manipulation. I am dinner for the next carnivorous, co-dependent, chemically desensitizing predator, with alcohol induced anger management issues, watching the next in a long line of them, play dangle the carrot with my food and security. I've watched people systematically turn a blind eye to my bruises, suffering & visible weakness from starvation.

In 2012, 3 days after Christmas I was weak from not eating for 5 days. I walked to a Baptist church in the snow and freezing cold in hopes of inspired direction, guidance. And, in hopes of something to eat to sustain my weakened body. I recall hearing parishioners speaking of how they were "so tired of eating turkey & leftovers." I humbly asked for something, anything to eat to sustain me. After the sermon, I was given coffee, a mug with the name of the church & couldn't understand being turned away as that congregation turned a blind eye to my bruises, weakness, and hunger. True to my upbringing, I politely thanked them as I realized that there would be no empathy or compassion for me that day. I was numb as I watched people turn a blind eye and keep on walking, I felt like the wounded, hungry man lying in the road that led from Jerusalem to Jericho in the parable of 'The Good Samaritan', (Acts 29.) Proverbs 27: 28, came to mind. It reads "He that giveth unto the poor shall not lack: but he that hideth his eyes shall have many a curse." I didn't wish that on those people. It seemed to me that they were already cursed. As I realized that, not unlike my abusers, those people were in prisons of their own choosing. Though having no family and having spent many holidays trapped in abuse, I don't recall ever feeling so alone in this world as I did that day. At least with my abusers, their words and actions were aligned and therefore more honest in that regard. I recall being envious of a stray cat that someone had fed that I passed on the side of the road. On my walk back to the shelter where I was staying, tears rolled down my face and my heart broken . I prayed for inspiration for the congregation that maybe a light in their heart might come on when the next hungry person crossed their path.

As much as I'd love to put the responsibility on my abusers, in my adult life, I alone made the executive decision to allow the emotional, physical and spiritual abuse to continue as long as it did.

I had watched my own Mother and role model accept this from men, which ultimately killed her. By the time that she became just another faceless statistic to die from DV, my 'foundation' was very cracked. I was already programmed that it was acceptable and must be 'what I deserved.' The emotionally masochistic seeds were planted and the toxic 'weeds' of anger, resentment, hostility and aggression were taking over 'my garden'. My cart of emotional baggage became heavier and heavier, to the point that I was exhausted, miserable and felt contempt for the woman who lived in my own mirror. The more I hated myself, the more the predators tried to 'rescue' and use me to serve their own agenda. After I had my face sliced and was run down with a car, the Hopi Indian Elder took me in and reprogrammed me HOW to forgive in order to heal - be free & FINALLY - 'Learn to Live.' It has been a long hard road. ~

I have faith that You will get there.

I have a feeling that You are much stronger than You think

For the past few years I've volunteered with ministries, working tirelessly to help counsel, bring awareness, and educate others of the signs, pitfalls to this vicious cycle of control & abuse.

Overcoming & healing begin with learning how to be honest with and about our-selves, making the conscientious choice to STOP playing the exhausting game of hide and seek from the demons who live in the mirror, in order to facilitate the clarity and healthy view of cause-effect. Seems that most of us are willing to settle for a life unlived, only to awaken one day when it's too late, with a stranger in our bed who has a familiar face and retrospectively look back at regretful conformist lives saying: woulda, coulda shoulda. When we finally come to our respective 'Crossroads' of life and those of us who've had ENOUGH must summon the courage of our convictions to pull the 'weeds' that have overtaken our 'garden'. When we can finally learn to be still and listen, we come to understand that it will take putting the fears and insecure ego on a shelf to gain the clarity to see through spiritual eyes, as opposed to carnal ones clouded by ego. When we walk towards the light, we gain the clarity of fresh eyes which will lead us out of the darkness that we've become conditioned to accept as our reality. As we then gain spiritual wisdom, we can finally discover the courage and freedom to heal from the obstacles from which we've been hiding all along. Then, at long last, we' find personal freedom the chains that bind us through enlightened grace.

I'm not here preaching hatred, anger, or vindication. When you've seen as much suffering as I have in my lifetime, you reach a point when you say - ENOUGH ! I fall to my knees in deep contrition and pray that the Great Spirit, that He will free me from the chains that bind me to the self deprecating cycle that systematically fulfills my own self defeating prophecies.

I never thought I'd ever be the one to preach forgiveness. In the process of my healing, after I left and was no longer a slave to the abuse, I was still imprisoned by my own anger, fears, insecurities, pain, resentment, bitterness , resentment , and personally, I've seen enough suffering for One lifetime. I had to forgive - for MYSELF, not for them. I feel nothing for them. And, the ONLY way that I would ever truly be free was to rise above, dig deeply & summon the strength to let it go. Not for my abusers, but to no longer be a prisoner of the atrocities which have scarred my soul. To truly be free, I'd have to take away their power. So, I wrote it all down on paper, put it in a red balloon, went to a mountaintop and let it go.

I do not forgive for them. That is a debt that everyone has to settle all on their own. I'm just saying that my cart of emotional baggage was getting exhaustingly heavy, and, until I came to a point in my life that I had seen enough suffering in the world and learned to let it go, they would always have power and control over me. Letting go of the pain, resentment, anger was the only way that I could ever truly be free.

For someone trapped in the vortex of abuse, we can ALL make a difference and be the answer to someone's prayer. Volunteer, donate, extend an Olive Branch, at least offer a warm embrace and an empathetic ear. But, please do not send the message of acceptance by being just another to mindlessly turn a blind eye, because we are in this together. I have freed myself of the chains that haunted me for so long, dug up my garden, and I am planting new seeds. Seeds that will be blossoming into beautiful flowering plants, that will sustain me for the rest of my life.

                                              Survivor: Elise Montgomery

*   *   *

In the mind of an abuser

The club, at the Naval base in Virginia Beach, was crowded with civilian women looking for a Sailor. Since it was either the 1st or 15th of the month , they knew that we just got paid and wanted to meet our acquaintance. I felt confident with myself, so I asked one lady to dance, even though I couldn't dance myself. Well, I guess she wasn't interested in me because I got shot down like a duck in hunting season. Normally, I would have been embarrassed and just walked away with my tail tucked between my legs, but I used the famous excuse that I've learned now is not an excuse and that was, "I was drunk." So, because of that 'excuse', I called that young lady a "Bitch" and I smacked her. It was one of the dumbest things that I have ever done, because she simply went right over to the Shore Patrol (Navy's military police) and I was arrested. While this was my first physical abuse against a woman, I was only charged with underage drinking and I've should have learned from that, but unfortunately my lack of learning lead to the emotional and physical pain to the very one I said I loved.

While I know now there is no reason for a man to raise their hand to a woman, there are excuses that abusers use to justify their violence. I'm only telling the story about myself, so I can't say that my "excuse" is every mans excuse. Power and control was something that I thought was the only cause of my anger. But I've recently learned, through counseling, that I have a fear of abandonment and it was this fear which gave me the wrong choices to make in my situations. It was these wrong choices that caused fear in my wife and actually within me. I will continue to state that there is no excuse for violence against a woman, yet I forced power and control against my wife because I was afraid of her. I was afraid she would find out that I was cheating. I was afraid that she would leave me. I was afraid that I was going to lose a really good wife. I was simply afraid of being alone. So, I thought that if I could intimidate her or scare her by wrapping my hands around her neck and placing some pressure on her neck, it would work and she wouldn't leave me and it would help me think of some creative lie to get out of my situations. Now, that was some creative language just to say that I choked her. But in my mind, I simply wanted her to know what could happen. While I can think of many instances of where I tried to scare my wife into complying with me, I'll never forget where my threats and even violence would not work.

Knowing that she was on the phone texting another man, I demanded for her to unlock her phone so that I could see. No matter how many times I demanded that she unlock the phone, she just wouldn't. I then straddled her on the bed, placed my hands around her neck and said in a calm voice,

"Go ahead and have [her daughter] call the police. It would take about 1 ½ minutes just to get the information to the dispatcher. About 30 seconds for the information to be dispatched. Another 30 seconds for the police to prepare to respond. And about 4 minutes for them to arrive. That's over 6 minutes to be rescued. Do you think you would still be living? Is your death and leaving your kids without a mother worth you not unlocking your phone?"

To my surprise, she still did not unlock the phone, I thought I could fool my wife into thinking that I was going to actually choke her, but she fooled me instead.

I only wanted to scare her and have that power to control her because I knew she was leaving me and I was afraid. "Don't piss me off" seemed to be my middle name. I would curse out my superiors in the U.S. Navy, co-workers at some of my various jobs, and of course in my marital relationships. Knowing that I have an anger problem, I continued counseling. In addition to my anger, I cheated on my wife. I didn't like the habit of having sex with other women while married. I hated that I ruined our marriage vows, so I knew this was a dilemma that I needed to fix. This is where I learned more about myself and the rationale for some of my behavior. After hours of counseling with therapists, psychologists, psychiatrists, and even clergy, I realized that my childhood had a direct correlation to my present behavior. Because of my mother's alcoholism, 3 which was rooted from depression, my mother abused me and I later lived with my father. Another pain that I had repressed and kept to only a few people was my incidence of sexual abuse at about the age of 5 by a family friend. On top of all of that, I was now diagnosed with major depression and trying to control my anger which made my home very tense and gave me more of an excuse to have power and control over my wife. During my abuse, my ultimate goal was "compliance." If I said that the moon was purple then you will have had to agree with me. It was my way, period.

It was during these times when my wife would stand her ground only to make me angrier. When the threats started flowing from the mouth of my wife in the form of sarcastic statements, deep inside I was scared, yet my choice of action was to strike back in the form of anger. "Maybe if I can scare her to listen, cooperate, or acknowledge me, I would be able to maintain control of my family." This was one of the thoughts that went through my head. Every time my wife would prevent me from obtaining my goal of superiority by ignoring me, walking away, yelling at me, and even hitting me herself, my mind only had the option to choose violence. I was too weak to make a positive choice, such as to walk away, talk, or even listen. Because I didn't think those methods would fix the problem as effectively as fear would. One day, I told my wife that I ran out of my depression medicine so I was feeling very depressed and volatile. Even though my wife knew how I could react without my medicine, she purposely called another man in the same room with me to make me angry. She became upset because she realized that I was talking to another woman on the phone. In fact, this woman was praying with me trying to save my marriage. As my wife begin to talk seductive to him over the phone, my heart began to race faster, my muscles began to stiffen, and I began to shake from anger. Remembering the things in counseling on how to control tense moments, my first step was to BREATHE. After a while, that didn't work, so my next step was to RE-EVALUATE. Which meant to think about what would happen if I would abuse her. I could possibly have my probation revoked, go to jail and lose my job as a fire fighter. When step 4 also failed to work, my final step was to LEAVE. I thought I was doing well because I'm controlling my anger, making the right choices, and doing what I was taught in counseling. But after taking two steps towards the front door, my wife made sure she got one more shot in and she gave a seductive laugh and whisper, "Yes!" to this man on the phone. Because of my weakness, I lost control to rationalize between right and wrong and chose wrong. As I demanded that my wife hang up the phone so that we could talk, she did so in an attempt to not let me see who she was talking to. Because my wife tried to avoid me, I snatched the phone from her and we tussled causing me to strike her head with the phone while fighting. While my intentions were not to physically harm her, I realized that I did anyway. But I do realize that I caused emotional abuse to her as well. Well, that was the straw that broke the camel's back. As I tried to talk to her, she refused and later left the house. Knowing that she would call the police, I grabbed a few things and I rushed out of the house. My wife later filed a police report and also filed a personal protection order. I never realized that she was preparing for this for some time. Because of my ways, she became the perfect model to R. Kelly's song, When a woman's fed up. There was truly nothing I could do to get her back. I later violated my PPO by contacting my wife and spent 30 days in jail. This was the beginning of a new chapter in both of our lives. Believing that I could still save my marriage, like a fool, I still tried to contact my wife begging her to talk but she refused. Since she is very close with my family, they informed me that she wants nothing to do with me. She began seeing another man even while I was in the hospital suffering from depression. I just could not believe that my wife would leave me like this knowing that I was desperately working on a positive change in my life. Because of so many factors within my life that I failed to control and failed in making the right decisions, I hurt the most beautiful woman in the world, disappointed my family, ruined my marriage, and made me less of a man, if a man at all, to those who were supposed to look up to me.

    I just explained the abuse that occurred during my last marriage, yet I was abusive in my first marriage, as well as when I dated my girlfriend who became the mother of my first child. I do not boast or brag about what I've done. Even though I have received God's forgiveness and ask forgiveness from those that I've abused, it took a long time for me to forgive myself. There are times, even while writing this, I feel so ashamed of what I did. However, after spending 30 days in jail, I reestablished my relationship with the Lord and with His guidance I am working hard everyday to prove that I am the man that God wants me to be. As I've said throughout my story, there is NO EXCUSE for a man to put their hands on you. Just as we make a CHOICE to harm, we can make a CHOICE not to harm. Never let a man say, "It was the beer that made me do it" or "I blackout". Stop thinking that YOU can change him because you can't. Only an abuser can change themselves. They have to seek help and truly want it. They have to realize the root cause of their abuse and emotionally uproot that horrible weed of abuse from their body.

    Many men try to cover up their problems with "I'm sorry", flowers, doing dishes for about a week, and being really nice. None of that matters, unless they KNOW why they do what they do. For me, I'm still uprooting my behavior of abuse, but so far I know that it has to do with being alone. I know that it has to do with my childhood. I know that it has to do with my mental state of mind. However, these are still NO EXCUSES for me to have made the wrong choices in life. Many have said, "What if she [my wife] was your daughter or sister?" Well let's assume that YOU are my daughter, sister, aunt, or friend. I would tell you to LEAVE! Do not stay in a relationship that you hope to save because you love him. Love does not cause pain. However, NEVER mention to him that you're going to leave him. NEVER mention that you're seeing someone else. Don't say anything that will make him think he's going to lose you. Yes, you may want to hurt him with words, but it's these words that may make him even more upset. Plan your exit with family, friends, police, and even domestic violence shelters. Once you get away, don't listen to the famous line, "Baby, baby please give me one more chance." There is certainly more advice through your local shelters and domestic violence organizations. But, my number one advice, is to prevent the abuse from ever happening. Learn a man's childhood. How were they with their parents? Did they grow up in an abusive home? Were they abused? These are just some of many things that you should learn from a man during the dating stage of your relationship. The purpose of telling my story was not to justify my actions or make me the victim. I wanted you to understand what goes on in my mind. A person that has abused.

I am truly sorry to every woman that has been a victim of domestic violence and I hope that reading my story will either get you the help that you need or prevent you from experiencing the harm that so many other women have experienced. There is not a day that goes by that I wish my wife (ex-wife) would come back to me. However, I remain focused on the Lord and I have Him direct my path into becoming a better man for someone else and myself. I know that the next time, God will ultimately be the head of my home and I will treat my wife like Christ loved the church. God Bless.

♚ Recovering Abuser: Brian C.

[Note: Brian's results are not typical of abusers, and it is important to know that, even though you hope this is the outcome of your abuser, chances are that they will continue to abuse you, getting worse the longer you stay. Get out and get the help that you need, regardless of the stories they tell you to get you to come back. Many abusers often use excuses and even admit they are wrong, to get you to return to them. Always be cautious of your abuser, they may put on a facade, just to regain their grip, and it could result in your death, or the death of those you love.]

* * *

There is no real way to begin a story like this. So let us begin shortly before I met my husband. I was a young 18 years old, barely legal, some would say. I would hang out with friends and family and help take care of my sick aunt. I had no real clue what life was like, even though I sure thought I did. I would go on dates, party with my friends, and fight with my mother. Wishing for more money, a bigger house, and new everything. I had my heart broken a couple of times but had great friends. I looked frequently for a job to make huge money for my mom, aunt and I, and one day I saw an AD for a traveling salesperson, "in a blue jean environment" for young adults with a $2,000 sign on bonus. I was quickly approaching my 19th birthday and decided to give them a call. I went through the phone interview and decided this is where my life needed to be, all the way in sunny California. It was like a dream, I've never been. I wanted to see the world and I was going to start there. I told one of my friends about the opportunity and he too came along for the ride hoping to support his own young family. They bought our bus passes and we were on our way to a new life.

Upon arriving there we soon discovered that the $2,000 we were promised was for room and board for 2 weeks while we learn the ropes of the company, We stayed in motels with an assigned roommate and mine was pretty cool, so I thought how nice this opportunity would be. I instantly fell in love with California, and knew some great things would happen there. The night we arrived I met my husband Randy. I liked him. He was quiet and shy and very timid. We chatted for a little while and I went off to my assigned room.

The next day I woke up rested from finally sleeping in a bed for the first time in five days. I did my makeup and hair, got dressed and went to a morning meeting. I could feel Randy's eyes on me the entire time. I liked that. We went out in the vans to make sales, which consisted of knocking on peoples doors and asking if they wanted to buy children's books. To train they put me with a guy who I learned was Randy's room mate, He asked me if I was interested to know more about anyone at the company. I said 'Yes, Randy'. He told me Randy was celibate and that he wasn't looking for any relationships and that he kept to himself. This was saddening because for some reason I had felt drawn to his quiet personality, shyness, and tattoos. Typical I know. Over the next few weeks I didn't talk with Randy much knowing he wasn't interested, and met another guy who was really nice, although I still had Randy on my mind. We started talking and I found out he had slept with a friend of mine that I had made. So I stopped talking to him and went on my way.

   We were off only on Sundays, and it was one of these Sundays that everyone was gone, either shopping or sightseeing, that I went to Randy's room knowing he was still at the hotel just like me. We started talking and found out we really had a lot in common, and I was even more drawn to him. We had our first kiss, and I was hooked. His roommate had been on vacation with his family at this time, so when he returned things changed. I came to find out that his roommate actually had interest in me and was jealous of Randy. He made Randy break up with me. That's when I found out that he had a power over Randy and would even take his money. I was heartbroken. I felt the need to take up for him. He was so quiet and loving….. I felt such a strong pull towards him and he felt the same, but he was allowing a random person to come between us.

  That night we changed to a new hotel, in Richmond California. and we worked the San Francisco area. I fought for Randy and told his roommate that is still wanted to talk to Randy, he finally gave in and set a strict set of rules for him. It was crazy, but I thought at least I would have Randy… We hung out all the time, had lunch together and just got to know each other. Our bosses and other couples on the company, would tease us about how cute a couple we were, and how crazy it was that Randy, the only one who never dated anyone, finally found someone worthy of him...

  I was very homesick, and wanted to leave, but wanted Randy to come back home with me to Atlanta. One day I woke up and said this was the day, I told Randy and we left together. I had enough money to get us a hotel for a week and we just went sightseeing right in San Francisco, We also had our first sexual encounter, and at the time it was amazing. He was still quiet and timid and I was really attracted to that. I couldn't believe he choose to come with me. It was the greatest feeling in the world. We arrived in Atlanta. We were broke but still in love and stayed with my mother. I was so happy.

  Things started changing little by little, old friends I had before I left for

California, couldn't come around, he would get angry and accuse me of having relationships with them. We were just friends but that didn't mean anything to him. He would say well they want to have sex with you not a friendship. We started fighting and quiet Randy was no more. A few months later I found out I was pregnant with my oldest son and I was so happy, and he seemed to be too. Soon after we found out I was pregnant, He would fight with me and tell me that they baby was not his. My mother and I fought just as much, to the point she kicked me out so many times I had enough and Randy and I left in the middle of the night in a cab and went to Charlotte to live with his mother. Things seemed to get better we had a few arguments here and there, and drove his mother crazy, but I still felt our love was strong enough to conquer all, and that it was normal.

I went to the hospital to be induced at 42 weeks, and was in labor for three days. At this point Randy was so stressed, We started arguing in the hospital, and he left with his mother, where on the way back home, they started to argue and he jumped from the moving vehicle. She called me crying saying Randy was run over by a truck, that was not true. However I'm in the hospital trying to have baby and they are acting like crazy idiots. Randy finally came back to the hospital, later that night and we had the baby a few hours later.

Needless to say he was never there for me when I needed him most. We brought the baby home from the hospital, and several days later, Randy would go across the street and get so drunk he would black out, leaving me to care for the baby by myself. One night he came home so angry, he was denying his child, and slapped me so hard and, pushed me down. He attempted to change a diaper that I had changed already, so he took the diaper he thought was soiled and smashed me in the face with it with all his might. He said 'How do you like that' I got up and grabbed the baby from him. Then he pushed us both down and I ended up having to throw the baby onto the bed, to prevent him from getting hurt.

His mother called the cops, but before they got there, I was sitting on the couch with the baby, He leaned over me, feeling his breath on my face. It smelled like strong liquor. He stayed there for a second and said 'don't say anything or this will be your end.' I was so scared for my baby I didn't say anything to the cops, and later called my mother who by that time had moved to Louisiana. She rushed to Charlotte in her truck and prepared to take me and the baby back with her. I allowed Randy to talk me into him coming with us saying it would never happen again and he was just drunk, accompanied with promises to never drink again. I believed him, and so he came with us. I honestly thought that he would never lay a hand on me again, Being my mother would never allow that to happen, and my child and I would be safe with her. That I loved him so much and, that I could love him out of this. Whatever it was. I could fix it.

Once we arrived in Louisiana, things were not much different. While I was pregnant, Randy did not work. The only thing that changed, was that he found a job soon after our arrival. He would get drunk after work. We would fight constantly, and he would especially fight with my mother's husband who was also an alcoholic. They eventually got into a fight that was so bad that we were forced to move into our own place where things seem to get a little better. He would still come home drunk and stay out too late drinking, we would fight sometimes, but everything seemed to be working out. I ended up getting pregnant again when my son was six months old. I was excited to be a mom again and he seemed excited too.

We started fighting and he would scream at me and come home drunk more frequently. When I was eight months pregnant with my second son, he threw a can of soda at my back, and I lost my breath. I tried to leave him and stayed at my mother's home for a few days and when he convinced me to come back, I realized he had bleached all my clothes, along with our, soon to be sons, clothes. It was heartbreaking. My clothes I could deal with, but my unborn child clothes broke me down big time. It was almost as if he kicked me in the stomach. It cut me deep and now I think I should have known then that he didn't really care. Those few days I was gone, he completely destroyed everything in the house, from pictures of our son and the wedding, to dishes, and furniture. He said he burned it all.

When I would cook dinner for him, he would say how horrible it was or I should've did something differently, and he would end up either throwing it away, or dumping it on me. I didn't know what he wanted me to be. I thought there must be something wrong with me, and that I needed to change or maybe it was just because he had a drinking problem. I encouraged him to get help for his drinking and he eventually did and he stopped drinking. I thought things would get better, but they didn't. It took me a long time to realize that anger and alcohol wasn't the problem. Randy had an abuse problem and the funny thing is, when we lived in Charlotte it was clear as day with all of his family. They were all abusive to their wives, and children. He held my eyes shut for so long..

While I was pregnant he quit his job and had no plans to get a new one. He then started to drink again and once I had my second son I returned to work. He never liked the fact that I had a job, nor did he believe I actually did something while I was there. I was always "Not about shit" or never good enough. Over the years I had several jobs where he accused me of cheating on him. When I was talking to coworkers or befriending them, and they would text me or call me and he would not approve because, they were either 'not married' or 'too young' and we were better than 'that'. I eventually had to quit these jobs because my home life would get continuously worse the longer I stayed at a job. This now hurts me because I have no real work history. He also did not want to work and who's going to buy diapers? It didn't matter what kind of job I had, it was never good enough for him. "It's not a real job" "it's not real work" etc.

One of the ways that I would constantly be abused numerous times a week, would be sexually. And I don't mean that he forced himself on me while I said no, I mean he would threaten to argue with me until the morning daylight if I did not consent to sex. And I'll tell you the entire time this was going on he did not want to wear condoms, nor would he even pick up my birth control. If I asked him to pick it up, he's too busy, or he forgot, or because he just didn't want to. On nights he wanted to 'make love' (that's what he called it) He would keep me up all night, arguing and then following me all around the house, just saying things to get under my skin. If I tried to go to sleep he would turn the light on, knowing the baby was asleep, telling me I'm worthless. Screaming about how I'm pathetic or trifling. How I must be cheating on him since I don't want to have sex or 'make love'. Throwing things and breaking phones and laptops. Whatever he could say or do to get a rise out of me that I would give in and have sex with him and be done. And that's what would happen. He would ask me to have sex I would say I'm too tired, or not tonight, tomorrow night and he would just argue me down until I allowed it to happen. And this made me really angry and resentful towards him. Towards the end all I could think about during sex with him, was how much I hated this person for doing this to me. I was disgusted not only in him, but in myself. And yes I ended up pregnant once again with my baby girl.

When I was pregnant the abuse did not stop, In fact, It got worse. He would throw things and yell 'Stupid fat bitch' 'Lazy motherfucker' on an almost daily basis. Randy never handled stress well. He would never stand a united front with me like husband and wife should. If well fell on hard times it was him against everyone. and I was the cause for it. He would never blame himself for quitting his job, instead it would be me. if something happened bad to us, like we get a flat tire or the CD player stopped working, It was my fault each time, and so the eggshells blanketed the floor.

Randy was very narcissistic. He loved himself, but hated everyone. Eventually he would find a way to blame someone other than himself, no matter who it was, for his awful behaviors and actions. Never once did I ever see him take responsibility for his own actions, And this contradicted everything my father taught me as a child, and made me even more ashamed to tell people about my situation.

I remember a time when I worked a short stint for a call center near my home. I made so many friends there, and even confided in some, but was afraid to tell Randy. In one of his good moods I invited a woman and her boyfriend to come over with her child for dinner and games, something we had never done before. He agreed and I was so excited. He had an attitude all night, and It really threw the whole evening off. I really liked this girl as a friend but every time she texted me Randy would throw a fit and make life miserable. Eventually, I had to cut ties with almost everyone I ever knew and quit many jobs I really enjoyed. The isolation was horrific and I was disturbed by it. I couldn't imagine ever having a healthy relationship with any friends or coworkers. Every day, upon my arrival at home, I would constantly check the clock in my van, to see what time, just in case he brought up what time I arrived. I was always later than I actually was, and each day he would ask what took me so long. That was an everyday struggle. The only reason I actually returned home was to make sure my children were ok. I remember several occasions if I had to work past 9:30 at night, he would just put the boys in their room, leaving dinner and baths for me to do when I returned from work. The kids would be hungry and needed changing. He was more concerned with drinking and watching porn on the internet to bother with them.

One morning I got up and ready for work, Randy had been up the entire night. I had to get up at 3:30 AM to pump before I got ready to leave. I had a shelf I was going to return to the store, because it was too small, after work. He was angry for another reason that I cannot recall. He took it out of the truck and throws it into the street, smashing it to pieces, pulls me from the truck, and starts pushing me around preventing me from getting back in the truck to go to work. He made me clean it up. Every piece. The entire time, screaming at me in the quiet street, waking up neighbors, I'm sure.

Once he allowed me to leave I was already late for work, and a crying mess. Once I arrived at work I made up some excuse for being late, and tried to act normal. I was asked to read something out loud, and while I was reading, my voice cracked and I started sobbing. I was so embarrassed. I blamed it on hormones from my pregnancy.

To this day I am still ashamed of the person I was when I was with him. I became a person I did not want to be, always lying for him, bottling things up, blaming myself for thing out of my control, and sometimes I would blame others. For example, whenever I would go to the store, I never felt like I could shop freely, I was always on a time limit. If I took 5 extra minutes, he would know. I would find myself getting short with cashiers, for taking too long, when really they were not. It was just the pressure of having to please someone else, to escape a beating, to prevent the harsh words that cut deep. No one should ever feel like this, like you cannot even get groceries for your family without having to account for each moment you spend, otherwise there would be hell to pay.

The abuse continued on almost a daily basis verbally. I would be called names in front of my children. Talked to like a dog. My pants would be pulled down to humiliate me. Food thrown at me objects thrown at me. His favorite thing to do was, pick up large objects while I was sitting down and act like he was going to hit me with them. I would almost always flinch, and he would laugh and set the object back down. This is a powerful tool they use, because it's almost as if they hit you. It still asserts power over you, but you feel as though you can't do anything about it, because he didn't hit you with it. Knifes would be pulled way too frequently for my taste, and a few of those times he would end up cutting himself to show the kind of damage he could do to me. I was frightened all the time, Never knowing when he would escalate the argument to something so deadly. Once we were driving with my oldest son and I was pregnant with my second, He was angry with me and started to drive erratically. He was swerving all over the road. He was trying to put fear into me… and it worked. Many times he would tell me he hopes I get raped, or sodomized, and even told me he was going to arrange for that to happen to me. I still look over my shoulder thinking he will keep true to his promise.

He would often threaten to kill himself if I ever leave. By dousing himself in gasoline setting himself on fire. He even threatened to burn me and the children alive in the house. His words were so powerful and he knew that. Thinking back now I have no idea how I was able to put up with that on an almost daily basis. It made me feel like I was nothing. Meaningless. Not good enough. I had all these hopes and dreams about keeping my family together. That I could love him through this. I knew he had a troubled past and background being sexually abused as a child. And I allowed myself to believe that this was the basis for his anger, hate, and abuse towards me.

When my oldest, was about two years old that's when I realized that there was a difference in how he treated the two boys. This was also the time that I realized that my son had autism. The way that he would discipline him for breaking a toy or for taking his diaper off, he would spank him, and scream at him with such anger and frustration. I couldn't understand why he would discipline a child so young in the way. He would often talk about "what ifs". Like "if my son ever did… I would beat the shit out of him" and I remember that would really make me angry because, here this is just a child, and it's going to be years and years before anything like this happens, or it could never happen. It was really frustrating for me because I couldn't quite understand why he would think in this way about our child. It was just about him, not any of the other children. I tried so hard to love my son a little more, and hug him a little tighter, and hold him a little closer to make up for the lack of love from his father. I would try to encourage Randy to get to know him, and play with him, and teach them things, but he showed little interest. I could tell that my son knew that his father showed him less love than the other children. If any of the other children did something wrong it always would turn out to be Bentlee's fault, and in turn he would be the one that was punished for it. I would ask him why, he would reply because he's the oldest. I never understood that. I was really upset with Randy for treating our oldest son this way. One time he hit Bentlee with truck tie downs and used it as a belt on his son. He would spank him and leave marks numerous amount of times. He once caught him by the back of the neck and left some very bad bruises on the back of his neck and head.

The last time he ever hit my son he slapped his leg with such force that it left three finger size whelps on his thigh. When I discovered the marks I was so shocked and I cried because you could see the anger that was left imprinted on his thigh. The abuse was also verbal for him as well. Calling him things like "Lazy" and "Retard" always saying in an underlining manner that he was not good enough to be his son. It got to the point where Bentlee would hide under his bed or in the corners of his room afraid that he was going to be yelled at. He would play so quietly, in fear that if he expressed his emotions in any way that he wanted to, that he was doing something wrong. My heart hurt for him. I didn't know what to do.

Looking back the 'Honeymoon' Phases of the relationship, it was very frequent and it gave me the illusion that things were going to be okay between us. I might get screamed at, I was hit, pushed, thrown, but the next day it was a different story I would get a foot rub, told how much I mean to him, a warm bath drawn, just overall treated so nice for a period of time. He knew how long that needed to last until the next abuse took place, each time worse than the last, just to keep me around. I have blocked so much of the abuse from my memory and tried not to think about how this has affected my mental state. But the truth can no longer be hidden in the shadows of my being. Its eating me alive from the inside, and the pain tears my heart. Every day, I remember something I've suppressed, and little by little I'm putting it in the light to shrivel and die there. My father always said the truth shall set you free, I've never know how true those words were until now.

The abuse over the years continue to escalate. It got so bad at times. One day we were arguing for hours we were trading horrible things back and forth he ended up smashing a lot of glass things on the floor where our children walk and crawl. I remember I was in the laundry room, and he was in the kitchen. Out of nowhere, he comes in and starts to strangle me with both of his hands with such force we fall back into our bedroom and I land on the back of my head, with him straddled on top of me, and he continued to strangle me pressed up against the floor. At this point I had hit my head so hard that I started slipping in and out of consciousness. I had tunnel vision and I could not breathe. All I could see was his face. That face was filled with such anger and hate. Teeth clenched.

I knew that I was going to die. I could see it in his eyes. I was prepared to die. With my children just a few feet away, I knew I would never see them again. I started to pass out, praying God would protect them from him. All of a sudden he got up and left when I got to my feet I was dizzy and choking in air. I knew what had happened to me but I didn't know who I was, or where I was. I didn't recognize anything around me, I started screaming "Where am I?" I ran around my house trying to find something I recognized, I grabbed a phone to call for help, he grabbed it from me and pushed me. I then blacked out. When I came to probably about 20 minutes later, I was sitting outside hyperventilating, and he was asking me if I was okay. All I could think about was my children. I started remembering everything then. I asked if the children were okay, and he said yes. My jaw felt broken because I couldn't swallow and I could not close my mouth. I told him I needed to go to the hospital. I called my mother to watch the children and I told her what had happened she was very angry, but was equally afraid of him. So she watched the children while he took me to the hospital. I told the doctors that I had memory loss and that I didn't remember what happened even though I did. The ER doctor told me that it looked exactly as if I had been strangled, but I just told him I didn't remember. They gave me a CAT scan and I didn't have any permanent jaw damage or head trauma that needed treatment immediately, so I was sent home. Even at the hospital he was blaming me for what happened. As if this, somehow, was still my fault that he had done this to me. I felt like I could have died had he had just strangled me a little longer, and at that time I almost wished he had. I now know that the prayer I said, to protect my children from him. Was answered when Randy released me right before I passed out. I know this happened because I am the one who was to protect them from him. If only I had realized that sooner.

I still didn't leave. I felt like I couldn't leave. I had three children to think about. What would happen to them? How would I be able to support them with no job, with no money, with nothing. It is the worst feeling in the world, to think you must live in hell to be able to have a place to sleep, and a warm bed for your children. Almost as if you are in a prison for doing nothing to get there. I would constantly ask myself what did I do to deserve this? I would tell myself I just needed to be a better wife, a better lover, a better cook, a better person. To do as I am told and things would be okay.

Little did I know, nothing but leaving would make this situation better, and even then there is a 50/50 chance of me surviving, knowing abusers become more violent when you attempt to leave. That is why you must have a plan.

A month later is when he left the whelps on my sons thigh. I woke up that morning to Randy saying "I'm going to kill them" and I knew he wasn't saying it in a literal sense however, he was angry. I got out of bed and so did he. I started to make breakfast and he went in there yelling at them to clean up their room. He came into the kitchen and started washing dishes and I went to their room to change their diapers, I pulled down my son's pants and discovered the marks on his thigh. I couldn't believe what I was seeing. I couldn't understand why he was spanked. What did he do wrong, besides wake up that morning. My heart swelled with such sadness for my son.

I knew then, like a light switch, that I had to do something before we were all killed or reached a point we could not return from. I went to the living room and retrieved my camera secretly. I then proceeded to take pictures of my sons thigh. I hid the camera with the pictures. And I said to Randy "What happened to Bentlee's leg?" He made me show him, because "I didn't do anything'. When I showed him he told me he 'didn't do that what do you mean?'. I couldn't believe that he even denied the fact that he did it. The he said 'he should have woke me up. 'He then stormed out of the house.

While he was gone I made some phone calls and call the domestic violence hotline number. A number I have called all too frequently but this time I was determined to find somebody to help me. I called and called and called some more, until I reached somebody who was willing to listen to me. I did not let the runaround phone system discourage me from breaking free of this abuse. I did not want it to last one second longer. I finally got in touch with a woman who listened to me, and was willing to help me find resources. She told me I had a few options. I could get my children and they would buy a bus ticket for me to move back to Atlanta, I could stay in my home and get a restraining order on Randy, or I could go to Lafayette to a women's shelter with my children. I didn't have any car insurance because he really wanted to keep me isolated so he stopped paying it so I couldn't go anywhere, and I didn't have any gas. So I had to wait until Thursday. Four whole days before I could do anything. She told me to think about my options and think about what would be best for me and the children, and to call her the next day with my decision. I chose to stay in my home and get a restraining order. Knowing the possibility that he could come back at any moment, because a restraining order is just a piece of paper, however I couldn't put my children in a shelter or on a bus for several days, knowing that if we did move to Atlanta we would not have anywhere to stay there either. So I made my decision, but I had to wait until Thursday. During those days I kept in contact with that woman, my advocate, and Randy knew something was off about me. I didn't want him to touch me. I didn't want to do what he wanted me to do. But I still had to play nice and that was the roughest thing I had to do. to continue to act like our relationship was okay. That we were moving forward so he wouldn't suspect anything and get angry with me and possibly hurt us. I'm not a very good liar, contrary to my adolescence.

During this time I spent a lot of time educating myself on domestic violence I realized that even though he was an alcoholic that wasn't the reason for the abuse. He had an abuse problem. It wasn't alcohol. It wasn't anger. It was abuse. The more I educated myself the more I started to realize that his narcissistic behaviors, his anger, his attitude towards little things, was just a perfect combination for the abuse. I started to realize that the abuse that I was going through was classic domestic violence and I never seen it in this light before. Ignorance is bliss.

On Thursday I loaded up my children in the car with no insurance and drove to the courthouse. Once we filled out the paperwork and had to go upstairs to have the judge sign off on it, the judge took one look at my children and knew they were victims of domestic violence just by their behavior. That was very heartbreaking to me. She didn't know my situation, but she knew the truth. Something that I had been trying to hide for years, she picked up on in a few seconds. She signed off on the restraining order for my children and I, but I still couldn't go home until he was served with the papers. We had to stay most of the night in a temporary shelter for women and children. It was almost like a jail. My kids were very stressed out, and didn't know where they were and they were very uncomfortable and cranky. I just sat and cried. I didn't know how I was going to make it had no money or anything. But I had my children, and they were safe, and I was safe. We were able to go home in the middle of the night and that was refreshing because I didn't know how I was going to sleep, or how the children were going to sleep in a place they were not familiar with. We came home and they went right to sleep. I was instantly relieved and just so happy that I was in my home and I didn't have to worry about him coming in yelling, screaming and hitting us. I felt happy for the first time.

I actually debated whether or not to get the restraining order up until the very last second I didn't know what I was going to do. I didn't know how I was going to be able to make it all I knew was I had to get my children safe. So that's what I did. He has tried to come back on several occasions, peeking through the windows and knocking on the door and each time I've had to call the police where they finally sent him to jail for a few days. Once we went to court I got the full restraining order, and custody of my children. I got the maximum 18 months of a protection order for my children and I, based on the evidence of abuse medical records and photographs. Divorce papers are soon to come as well. I just got approved for legal aid, and they just passed a law where I can possibly be granted an immediate divorce, based on the circumstances.

We now still live in our home where much of the abuse took place. Those are sad memories however we are building happier ones, I'm still struggling financially, but to me that struggle is so much easier than the life struggle. Knowing I will wake up alive and well, and my children will wake up alive and well, God willing, is far greater a blessing, than anything monetary. I thank God every day for this new life that he's given me and my children. I'm so thankful that I lived through it, and my children have a mother who loves them so much. You never know how strong you really are until you are put in a situation where you actually have to be strong. And we are getting stronger every day. I will continue to do everything in my power to keep them safe and out of harm's way. We create our children's hell. I will not allow my children to grow up and think that abusing, or being abused is okay, or healthy. And I sleep well at night knowing that I no longer subject them to that type of behavior. I can love them through this.

❀ **Survivor: Amberlee Hoagland**

* * *

Statistics:

The Victims

1 in 4 women will experience domestic violence during her lifetime.

Women experience more than 4 million physical assaults and rapes because of their partners, and men are victims of nearly 3 million physical assaults.

Women are more likely to be killed by an intimate partner than men.

Women ages 20 to 24 are at greatest risk of becoming victims of domestic violence.

Every year, 1 in 3 women who is a victim of homicide is murdered by her current or former partner.

The Families

Every year, more than 3 million children witness domestic violence in their homes.

Children who live in homes where there is domestic violence also suffer abuse or neglect at high rates (30% to 60%).

A 2005 Michigan study found that children exposed to domestic violence at home are more likely to have health problems, including becoming sick more often, having frequent headaches or stomachaches, and being more tired and lethargic.

A 2003 study found that children are more likely to intervene when they witness severe violence against a parent – which can place a child at great risk for injury or even death.

The Circumstances

Domestic violence is most likely to occur between 6 pm and 6 am.

More than 60% of domestic violence incidents happen at home.

The Consequences

According to the U.S. Department of Housing and Urban Development, domestic violence is the third leading cause of homelessness among families.

In New York City, 25% of homeless heads of household became homeless due to domestic violence.

Survivors of domestic violence face high rates of depression, sleep disturbances, anxiety, flashbacks, and other emotional distress.

Domestic violence contributes to poor health for many survivors. For example, chronic conditions like heart disease or gastrointestinal disorders can become more serious due to domestic violence.

Among women brought to emergency rooms due to domestic violence, most were socially isolated and had fewer social and financial resources than other women not injured because of domestic violence.

Without help, girls who witness domestic violence are more vulnerable to abuse as teens and adults.

Without help, boys who witness domestic violence are far more likely to become abusers of their partners and/or children as adults, thus continuing the cycle of violence in the next generation.

Domestic violence costs more than $37 billion a year in law enforcement involvement, legal work, medical and mental health treatment, and lost productivity at companies.

Most domestic violence incidents are *never* reported.

Help change the facts. Speak up, speak out, and make a difference for victims of domestic violence.

Safety Plan:

✻ During an argument, or tension building, stay in a room with no weapons and two exits.

✻ Locate your best escape route in an emergency.

Know where you would go in an emergency, have a plan.

✻ Locate any weapons and remove, hide, and unload them.

✻ Pack and hide an emergency bag

✻ Be careful about telephone and internet use. clear browser and internet history.

✻ Abusers and radial, and learn where you are going.

✻ Safety plan for children: Arrange a safe place for a child to run for help.

✻ Teach children how to dial 911, arrange a code word to let them know when to call or when to run and hide.

✻ ✻ ✻

When I leave I should Have:

✻ Identification for myself

✻ Children's birth certificates

✻ My birth certificate

✻ Social Security Cards

✻ School and Vaccination records

Printed in Great Britain
by Amazon